Series / Number 07-045

# LINEAR PROBABILITY, LOGIT, AND PROBIT MODELS

**JOHN H. ALDRICH**
*University of Minnesota*

**FORREST D. NELSON**
*University of Iowa*

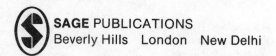

**SAGE** PUBLICATIONS
Beverly Hills   London   New Delhi

*For information address:*

SAGE Publications, Inc.
275 South Beverly Drive
Beverly Hills, California 90212

SAGE Publications India Pvt. Ltd.
C-236 Defence Colony
New Delhi 110 024, India

SAGE Publications Ltd
28 Banner Street
London EC1Y 8QE, England

International Standard Book Number 0-8039-2133-0

Library of Congress Catalog Card No. 84-051766

FIRST PRINTING

When citing a professional paper, please use the proper form. Remember to cite the
correct Sage University Paper series title and include the paper number. One of the
following formats can be adapted (depending on the style manual used):

(1) IVERSEN, GUDMUND R. and NORPOTH, HELMUT (1976) "Analysis of
Variance." Sage University Paper series on Quantitative Applications in the Social
Sciences, 07-001. Beverly Hills and London: Sage Pubns.

*OR*

(2) Iversen, Gudmund R. and Norpoth, Helmut. 1976. *Analysis of Variance.* Sage
University Paper series on Quantitative Applications in the Social Sciences, series no.
07-001. Beverly Hills and London: Sage Pubns.

# CONTENTS

**Series Introduction**  5

**Acknowledgments**  7

**1. The Linear Probability Model**  9

   1.0   Introduction  9
   1.1   Review of the Multivariate, Linear Regression Model  10
   1.2   A Dichotomous Dependent Variable and the Linear Probability Model  12
   1.3   A Dichotomous Response Variable with Replicated Data  20
   1.4   Polytomous or Multiple Category Dependent Variables  22
   1.5   The Linearity Assumption  24
   1.6   The Effect of an Incorrect Linearity Assumption  27

**2. Specification of Nonlinear Probability Models**  30

   2.0   Introduction  30
   2.1   The General Problem of Specification  30
   2.2   Alternative Nonlinear Functional Forms for the Dichotomous Case  31
   2.3   Derivation of Nonlinear Transformations from a Behavioral Model  35
   2.4   Nonlinear Probability Specifications for Polytomous Variables  37
   2.5   Behavior of the Logit and Probit Specifications  40
   2.6   Summary  47

3. **Estimation of Probit and Logit Models for Dichotomous Dependent Variables  48**
    3.0   Introduction  48
    3.1   Assumptions of the Models  48
    3.2   Maximum Likelihood Estimation  49
    3.3   Properties of Estimates  52
    3.4   Interpretation of and Inference from MLE Results  54
    3.5   Conclusions  65

4. **Minimum Chi-Square Estimation and Polytomous Models  66**
    4.0   Introduction  66
    4.1   Minimum Chi-Square Estimation for Replicated, Dichotomous Data  67
    4.2   Polytomous Dependent Variables  73

5. **Summary and Extensions  78**
    5.0   Introduction  78
    5.1   Summary  78
    5.2   Extensions  81

**Notes  85**

**References  93**

**About the Authors  95**

## Series Editor's Introduction

Earlier in this series, we published papers on regression analysis by Lewis-Beck and by Achen. Picking up where these papers left off, Nelson and Aldrich develop the logit and probit models analyzing dependent variables which are not continuous. Although there has been a tendency for many social scientists who analyze dichotomous dependent variables, such as vote choice, to simply proceed with ordinary regression analysis, Nelson and Aldrich show that this is really not an appropriate strategy. Probit analysis is more ideally suited to such problems, and, in the general case of polytomous dependent variables, logit ought to be the method of choice.

Aldrich and Nelson review the linear probability model, and then introduce the reader to several alternative specifications of nonlinear models, including the normal, logistic, Gompertz, Burr, and several others. The remainder of the monograph is devoted to the discussion of the estimation of probit and logit models, the assumptions of these models, and problems of inference. The authors use several examples to demonstrate the differences among the linear, logit and probit models, and to illustrate the importance of various assumptions in these models.

Although the material covered here is inherently difficult for many social scientists, the authors have done quite a good job of presenting formal statements followed by verbal translations followed by detailed examples. This pedagogic strategy should serve the neophyte well, and this of course is the intention of our series of monographs. The topic—probit and logit models—is not an introductory one. The reader should have a good understanding of linear regression analysis and of statistical inference. But for such readers, the presentation of this *topic* is an introductory one, and we fully expect that this monograph will have the effect of increasing the usage of logit and probit models in social science disciplines such as sociology, psychology, political science, and perhaps others as well. It has been aimed directly at the economics market, of course, and should provide a readable and lucid introduction for economists who, as a group, already make considerable use of logit and probit models. As such, this paper represents the first in a series of publications that we intend to present for the econometrics market. In so doing, we hope to provide a service supplementing the standard econometrics textbooks, and also provide a vehicle to upgrade statistical methodology in the other social science disciplines. Many graduate students in social sciences other than economics often have great difficulty mastering a standard econometrics text, and it is our hope that by presenting some topics in econometrics in our series, we can provide a bridge between standard econometrics and other social science treatments of statistical concepts. We find this manuscript to be an excellent choice as an initial move in this direction, because the presentation is so well done and because it has received rave reviews from some of the best econometricians.

—*John L. Sullivan*
Series Co-Editor

## Acknowledgments

We would like to thank Professors Lee Spector and Michael Mazzeo for making their data available for our use, Professor Raymond Duvall and two referees for their useful comments, and Professors John Sullivan and Richard Niemi, editors, and Sage Publications for their support. We alone remain responsible for remaining errors.

# LINEAR PROBABILITY, LOGIT, AND PROBIT MODELS

**JOHN H. ALDRICH**
*University of Minnesota*
**FORREST D. NELSON**
*University of Iowa*

## 1. THE LINEAR PROBABILITY MODEL

### 1.0 Introduction

Regression analysis has become a standard statistical tool in the social sciences. Its popularity stems from several sources. It provides much explanatory power, especially due to its multivariate nature. The Gauss-Markov Theorem (Johnston, 1984) proves that it has some very desirable statistical properties. It is widely available in computer packages, it is easy to interpret, and there is a widespread belief that it remains a reasonable procedure even if some of the assumptions underlying it are not met in the data (a property statisticians refer to as "robustness").

Perhaps because of its widespread popularity, regression may be one of the most abused statistical techniques in the social sciences. While estimates derived from regression analysis may be robust against errors in some assumptions, other assumptions are crucial, and their failure will lead to quite unreasonable estimates. Such is the case when the dependent variable is a qualitative measure rather than a continuous, interval measure. After reviewing the linear regression model, we shall show that regression estimates with a qualitative dependent variable can lead to serious errors in inference. For example, we shall show that regression estimates with a qualitative dependent variable may seriously misestimate the magnitude of the effects of independent variables, that all of the standard statistical inferences such as hypothesis tests or the

9

construction of confidence intervals are unjustified, and that the regression estimates will be highly sensitive to the range of particular values observed for the independent variables (thus making extrapolations or forecasts beyond the range of the data especially unjustified).

The failure of multivariate regression with a qualitative dependent variable is particularly troubling in the behavioral sciences, for many of the behaviors of interest, as well as attitudes and preferences underlying them, are qualitative—or at least observed qualitatively. Voting, for example, is one of the key variables in political science. In economics, individual choices to sell or to purchase a good, to enter a contract, and so on, are central problems. In sociology, one might be concerned with the decision to marry, to go to college, to have children, or any number of other qualitative choices. All of these behaviors are qualitative, often representing even dichotomous decisions. Many attitudes may be measurable in only a small number of categories. Party affiliation, ideology, the importance of religion in one's life, and many others may be potentially quantitative attitudes, but in practice are often measured qualitatively, especially in large surveys. What is needed, therefore, is some set of statistical techniques that can do the work of multivariate regression but that are not subject to its liabilities in the presence of qualitative dependent variables. Fortunately, several such procedures exist, and the purpose of this volume is to present some of them.

In this chapter, we will build the case that they are needed. The first section presents a quick review of the linear regression model, presenting notation, assumptions, and central results (see Lewis-Beck, 1980, and Achen, 1982 in this series for more details). The second section considers the use of regression with a dichotomous dependent variable. Section three and four extends the analysis when the dichotomous dependent variable is repeatedly observed and when it is polytomous (i.e., qualitative but with more than two categories), respectively. Section five examines the linearity assumption, and section six covers some of the errors of inference that may arise from assuming it incorrectly.

## 1.1 Review of the Multivariate, Linear Regression Model

A regression equation with, say, two independent (aka exogenous)[1] variables may be written;

$$Y_i = b_1 + b_2X_{i2} + b_3X_{i3} + u_i$$

or, in the general case, using summation notation:[2]

$$Y_i = \Sigma b_kX_{ik} + u_i \qquad [1.1]$$

In 1.1, Y is the dependent variable, $X_k$ for $k = 2, \ldots, K$ are the exogenous or independent variables, u is the random error (or disturbance term) which is, of course, unobserved, $b_k$ are unknown constants,[3] and the subscript i denotes the $i^{th}$ observation from the sample of size N.

In 1.1, we observe only $Y_1$ and $X_{ik}$, the values in the sample for the dependent and independent variables. The central problem is to estimate the unobserved constants or parameters, $b_k$. Let the parameter estimates be denoted by $\hat{b}_k$. Replacing the $b_k$ in 1.1 with $\hat{b}_k$ yields

$$Y_i = \Sigma \hat{b}_k X_{ik} + e_i \qquad [1.2]$$

This equation may be rearranged to solve for the error term:

$$e_i = Y_i - \hat{b}_k X_{ik} \qquad [1.3]$$

Squaring equation 1.3 and summing over all N observations yields the sum of squared errors. The ordinary least squares (OLS) estimates of the $b_k$ are those which minimize that sum.[4] Elementary calculus is used to find the minimum. So doing yields K equations, one for each of the unknown $b_k$'s. To solve K equation for K unknowns, $\hat{b}_k$, requires that each equation not be an exact linear combination of any of the others. But what this means is that the independent variables are not perfectly collinear, the first assumption of OLS regression. At the very least, that requires at least as many observations as there are parameters to estimate (i.e., $N \geq K$).

To this point, we have not discussed specification of the equation. Unless otherwise noted, we assume throughout, as users of regression assume, that all relevant—and no irrelevant—X's have been included in the equations 1.1 and 1.2 (see Lewis-Beck, 1980; Achen, 1982, for more details).

The remaining assumptions concern the disturbance term $u_i$.[5] Possibly the most important of these assumptions is that $u_i$ is not correlated with any of the independent variables, $X_k$, and that it has a mean of zero (assumption 3a and 3d in Lewis-Beck, 1980, p. 26). This implies that, given the $X_i$, the mean, or expected value, of $Y_i$ is

$$E(Y_i | X_{i1}, \ldots X_{ik}) = \Sigma b_k X_{ik} \qquad [1.4]$$

If so, then the OLS solutions, $\hat{b}_k$, will be unbiased estimators of the unknown parameters of interest, $b_k$.

The last two assumptions made about $u_i$ are it has a constant variance, $\sigma_u^2$, across all observations, and that it is uncorrelated from one observation to another. These two are called "homoscedasticity" and "serial independence," respectively. The set of three assumptions about $u_i$ are often called the Gauss-Markov assumptions, because they are those used in the Gauss-Markov Theorem. This theorem states that, given this set of assumptions, the OLS estimators are the best (most "efficient" in the sense of having the smallest sampling variance) estimators of those which are linear (in $Y_i$) and unbiased—so-called "BLUE" for "best," linear, unbiased estimator. It is easy to construct an unbiased estimator of the variance of the disturbance term $\sigma_u^2$:

$$S_u^2 = \Sigma e_i^2 / (N-K)$$

This statistic is closely related to the F statistic and $R^2$ which provide checks on the overall fit of the model.

A final common assumption is that $u_i$ is normally distributed. That implies that $\hat{b}_k$ are normally distributed. Finally, the sampling variances of the $\hat{b}_k$'s ($s_k^2$ as estimators of $\sigma_k^2$) can be computed, and their distributions known. From these, hypothesis tests can be constructed, confidence intervals computed, and so on.

## 1.2 A Dichotomous Dependent Variable and the Linear Probability Model

The regression model places no restrictions on the values that the independent (exogenous) variables take on, except that they not be exact linear combinations of each other. They may be continuous, interval level (net worth of a company), they may be only positive or zero (percent of vote a party received), they may be integers (number of children in a family), or they may be dichotomous (so-called dummy variables, e.g., scored as a one if make, zero if female).

The dependent variable, however, is assumed to be continuous. Since there are no restrictions on the $X_k$'s, the $b_k$'s, or the $u_i$'s, then $Y_i$ must be free to take on any value from negative infinity to positive infinity. In practice, $Y_i$ will take on only a small set of values in the data. For example, even if $Y_i$ is family income for the year, only a relatively small range of values will be observed. But, in this case, since any $X_k$'s will be similarly restricted, the assumption of continuous, interval measurement of $Y_i$ will not be a bad approximation. But, if $Y_i$ can take on only two values (say zero and one), the violation of this assumption is so egregious as to merit special attention.

Suppose $Y_i$ equals either zero or one. The expected value of $Y_i$ reduces to the probability that $Y_i$ equals one [symbolized as $P(Y_i = 1)$]:

$$E(Y_i) = 1 \cdot P(Y_i = 1) + 0 \cdot P(Y_i = 0) = P(Y_i = 1) \qquad [1.5]$$

If we then combine equations 1.4 and 1.5, we get

$$E(Y_i) = P(Y_i = 1) = \Sigma b_k X_{ik} \qquad [1.6]$$

From this we conclude that the right-hand side of the regression equation must be interpretable as a probability, i.e., restricted to between zero and one. For this reason, a linear regression model with a dependent variable that is either zero or one is called the linear probability model or LPM.

If $Y_i$ takes on only two values, then $u_i$ can assume only two values itself, for any given values of $X_{ik}$. That is, by equation 1.1 for $Y_i$ equalling zero and one, respectively, we get:

$$\text{If } Y_i = 0, \text{ then } (0 = \Sigma b_k X_{ik} + u_i) \text{ or } (u_i = -\Sigma b_k X_{ik})$$
$$\text{If } Y_i = 1, \text{ then } (1 = \Sigma b_k X_{ik} + u_i) \text{ or } (u_i = 1 - \Sigma b_k X_{ik}) \qquad [1.7]$$

Now, it can be shown that the first key assumption about $u_i$, that its expectation be zero, can be maintained:

$$E(u_i) = P(Y_i = 0)\,[-\Sigma b_k X_{ik}] + P(Y_i = 1)\,[1 - \Sigma b_k X_{ik}]$$

$$= -[1 - P(Y_i = 1)]\,P(Y_i = 1) + P(Y_i = 1)\,[1 - P(Y_i = 1)] = 0$$

As a result, OLS estimates of $b_k$ will be unbiased. However, the assumption that the $u_i$ have a constant variance cannot be maintained. In fact, the variance of $u_i$ varies systematically with the values of the independent variables.

$$v(u_i) = E(u_i^2) = P(Y_i = 0)\,[-\Sigma b_k X_{ik}]^2 + P(Y_i = 1)\,[1 - \Sigma b_k X_{ik}]^2$$

$$= [1 - P(Y_i = 1)]\,[P(Y_i = 1)]^2 + P(Y_i = 1)\,[1 - P(Y_i = 1)]^2$$

$$= P(Y_i = 1)\,[1 - P(Y_i = 1)]$$

$$= [\Sigma b_k X_{ik}]\,[1 - \Sigma b_k X_{ik}]$$

Thus, the OLS estimate, $\hat{b}_k$, will be unbiased but not best (i.e., not have the smallest possible sampling variance). As a further result, estimates of the sampling variances will not be correct, and any hypothesis tests (e.g., the t and F tests) or confidence intervals based on these sampling variances will be invalid, even for very large samples. Thus, even in the best circumstances, OLS regression estimates of a dichotomous dependent variable are, although unbiased, not very desirable. There is, however, a solution to this problem that is a fairly simple modification of OLS regression.

### 1.2.1 WLS ESTIMATION TECHNIQUE FOR
### THE LINEAR PROBABILITY MODEL

Goldberger (1964) proposed a two-step, weighted estimator to correct the problems of OLS regression of the linear probability model. The first step is to do the usual OLS regression of $Y_i$ on the $X_{ik}$. So doing yields the unbiased estimates $\hat{b}_k$. From these estimates, construct the set of weights, one for each observation:

$$w_i = [1/(\Sigma \hat{b}_k X_{ik})(1 - \Sigma \hat{b}_k X_{ik})]^{1/2} \qquad [1.8]$$

These weights are just the reciprocals of the estimated standard errors of $u_i$. Now multiply both sides of eq. 1.1 by $w_i$:

$$(w_i Y_i) = \Sigma(\hat{b}_k w_i X_{ik}) + (w_i u_i) \qquad [1.9]$$

It can be shown (Goldberger, 1964), that $(w_i u_i)$ has a constant variance, so that regressing $(w_i Y_i)$ on $(w_i X_{ik})$ by OLS yields new estimates, say $\tilde{b}_k$, which are not only unbiased but also have the smallest possible sampling variances. The standard errors of the second set of estimates, $\tilde{b}_k$, are the correct ones for conducting hypothesis tests, and the like.[6] Finally, $u_i$, taking on but two values, cannot be normally distributed. However, in large samples, $\tilde{b}_k$ turn out to be approximately normally distributed, so that hypothesis tests and the like can be used in the usual manner.

The only statistic resulting from the second stage estimation not of much use is the $R^2$. The one computed at this stage correctly reports the proportion of variance explained, but the variance referred to is the variance of the weighted dependent variable, not the original one. The $R^2$ could be recomputed from the untransformed data according to the formula

$$R^2 = \left[1 - \overset{N}{\underset{i}{\Sigma}}(Y_i - \overset{k}{\underset{k}{\Sigma}}\tilde{b}_k X_{ik})\right]^2 / \overset{N}{\underset{i}{\Sigma}}(Y_i - \bar{Y})^2$$

where $\tilde{b}_k$ represents the WLS coefficient estimates, $Y_i$ and $X_{ik}$ are the original data, and $Y$ is the sample mean of the $Y_i$. But even this quantity is of limited use for at least two reasons. First, since the $Y_i$ are inherently heteroscedastic, even computing a sample variance is like adding apples and oranges, and the statistical interpretation of the fraction of this aggregation explained is imprecise at best. Second, since OLS has the property of maximizing the $R^2$, the quantity computed as above is guaranteed to be smaller than the OLS $R^2$, leading to another interpretive quandary—generally we prefer models with the highest $R^2$, but here we know, on theoretical grounds, that a model with lower $R^2$ is preferred. Given these difficulties, use of the coefficient of determination as a summary statistic should be avoided in models with qualitative dependent variables.

What we have done, therefore, is to describe a procedure for valid estimation of a linear regression equation in the face of a dichotomous dependent variable—so long as the new assumption about the disturbance term (following from equation 1.7) can be made. Clearly, the implications of this assumption are very different from the usual assumptions made in OLS regression. The $u_i$ are not assumed to be continuous, homoscedastic or normally distributed. Rather, they are assumed to be *dichotomous and dependent upon the parameters, $b_k$, and values of the independent variables.*

### 1.2.2 AN EXAMPLE

Spector and Mazzeo (1980) examined the effect of a teaching method denoted as PSI on the performance of students in a course, intermediate macro economics. The question was whether students exposed to the method scored higher on exams in the class. They collected data on students from two classes, one in which PSI was used and another in which traditional teaching methods were employed. Those data are reproduced in Table 1.1 and include for each of 32 students the entering grade point average (GPA), the score on an exam given at the beginning of the term to test entering knowledge of the material (TUCE), a dummy variable indicating teaching method (PSI), and the final grade, recorded here as 1 for an A and 0 for a B or C (GRADE). GRADE is the dependent variable, and of particular interest is whether PSI has a significant influence on GRADE. Casual inspection of the data reveals a high correlation between PSI and GRADE—eight of fourteen students taught by the PSI method earned A's while only three of eighteen non-PSI students received A's. But TUCE and GPA are also positively related to GRADE. Students earning an A had an average GPA of 3.43, while other students averaged only 2.95, for example. And those taught by the PSI method had, on average, slightly higher GPAs and TUCE scores. A multivariate analysis is required to ascertain whether the

**TABLE 1.1**

**Data on the Effect of "Personalized System of Instruction" (PSI) on Course Grades**

| OBS PSI | GPA Grade | TUCE Grade | PSI | Grade | Letter Grade | OBS PSI | GPA Grade | TUCE Grade | PSI | Grade | Letter Grade |
|---|---|---|---|---|---|---|---|---|---|---|---|
| 1 | 2.66 | 20 | 0 | 0 | C | 17 | 2.75 | 25 | 0 | 0 | C |
| 2 | 2.89 | 22 | 0 | 0 | B | 18 | 2.83 | 19 | 0 | 0 | C |
| 3 | 3.28 | 24 | 0 | 0 | B | 19 | 3.12 | 23 | 1 | 0 | B |
| 4 | 2.92 | 12 | 0 | 0 | B | 20 | 3.16 | 25 | 1 | 1 | A |
| 5 | 4.00 | 21 | 0 | 1 | A | 21 | 2.06 | 22 | 1 | 0 | C |
| 6 | 2.86 | 17 | 0 | 0 | B | 22 | 3.62 | 28 | 1 | 1 | A |
| 7 | 2.76 | 17 | 0 | 0 | B | 23 | 2.89 | 14 | 1 | 0 | C |
| 8 | 2.87 | 21 | 0 | 0 | B | 24 | 3.51 | 26 | 1 | 0 | B |
| 9 | 3.03 | 25 | 0 | 0 | C | 25 | 3.54 | 24 | 1 | 1 | A |
| 10 | 3.92 | 29 | 0 | 1 | A | 26 | 2.83 | 27 | 1 | 1 | A |
| 11 | 2.63 | 20 | 0 | 0 | C | 27 | 3.39 | 17 | 1 | 1 | A |
| 12 | 3.32 | 23 | 0 | 0 | B | 28 | 2.67 | 24 | 1 | 0 | B |
| 13 | 3.57 | 23 | 0 | 0 | B | 29 | 3.65 | 21 | 1 | 1 | A |
| 14 | 3.26 | 25 | 0 | 1 | A | 30 | 4.00 | 23 | 1 | 1 | A |
| 15 | 3.53 | 26 | 0 | 0 | B | 31 | 3.10 | 21 | 1 | 0 | C |
| 16 | 2.74 | 19 | 0 | 0 | B | 32 | 2.39 | 19 | 1 | 1 | A |

SOURCE: Spector and Mazzeo (1980).

PSI-GRADE relation is independent of or in addition to other factors, or whether the apparent positive relation is spurious. Thus GPA and TUCE are included in the analysis to control for ability and background.

Results of a simple OLS regression on these data are presented in Table 1.2a. Except for the coefficient estimates and descriptive statistics, the results appearing there are not of much use for the reason noted above—the heteroscedastic residuals. To proceed with the weighted least squares analysis, the weights must be constructed using the co-efficient estimates of Table 1.2a. Define the variable $\hat{Y}_i$ according to

$$\hat{Y}_i = -1.498 + .4638*GPA(i) + .3785*PSI(i) + .0105*TUCE(i)$$

Then the weights (w) are determined according to

$$w_i = 1/[(\hat{Y}_i)(1 - \hat{Y}_i)]^{1/2}$$

Each variable, including the intercept, is then multiplied by this weight, and OLS is applied to the transformed variables.[7]

Results of the weighted least squares analysis are reported in Table 1.2b. (The descriptive statistics reported there are for the transformed

## TABLE 1.2a
### Ordinary Least Squares Results on PSI Data

| | | Descriptive Statistics | | Standard |
| | | Sum | Mean | Deviation |
|---|---|---|---|---|
| Grade | | 11.0 | 0.3437 | 0.4826 |
| GPA | | 99.75 | 3.117 | 0.4667 |
| PSI | | 14.0 | 0.4375 | 0.5040 |
| TUCE | | 702.0 | 21.94 | 3.902 |

| Model: | MODEL01 | SSE | 4.216474 | F Ratio | 6.65 |
|---|---|---|---|---|---|
| Weight: | 1/ (P (1-P) ) | DFE | 28 | Prob > F | 0.0016 |
| Dependent | | | | | |
| Variable: | Grade | MSE | 0.150588 | R-Square | 0.4159 |

| Variable | DF | Parameter Estimate | Standard Error | T Ratio | Prob > \|T\| |
|---|---|---|---|---|---|
| Intercept | 1 | −1.498 | 0.5239 | −2.859 | 0.0079 |
| GPA | 1 | 0.4639 | 0.1620 | 2.864 | 0.0078 |
| PSI | 1 | 0.3786 | 0.1392 | 2.720 | 0.0111 |
| TUCE | 1 | 0.0105 | 0.0195 | 0.539 | 0.5944 |

## TABLE 1.2b
### Weighted Least Squares Results on PSI Data

| | | Descriptive Statistics | | Standard |
| | | Sum | Mean | Deviation |
|---|---|---|---|---|
| Grade | | 97.377 | 0.0179 | 1.756 |
| GPA | | 15051.41 | 2.767 | 2.384 |
| PSI | | 122.56 | 0.0225 | 1.966 |
| TUCE | | 97018.4 | 17.83 | 41.48 |

| Model: | MODEL02 | SSE | 22.739 | F Ratio | 29.92 |
|---|---|---|---|---|---|
| Weight: | 1/(P (1-P) | DFE | 28 | Prob > F | 0.0001 |
| Dependent | | | | | |
| Variable: | Grade | MSE | 0.8121 | R-Square | 0.7622 |

| Variable | DF | Parameter Estimate | Standard Error | T Ratio | Prob > \|T\| |
|---|---|---|---|---|---|
| Intercept | 1 | −1.309 | 0.2885 | −4.536 | 0.0001 |
| GPA | 1 | 0.3982 | 0.08783 | 4.533 | 0.0001 |
| PSI | 1 | 0.3878 | 0.1052 | 3.687 | 0.0010 |
| TUCE | 1 | 0.0122 | 0.0045 | 2.676 | 0.0123 |

variables, GPA*W, INTERCEPT*W, and so on. Comparing the OLS and WLS results, note that the coefficient estimates change but not by much—the only problem with OLS estimates is high sampling variance. All other results, on the other hand, are markedly different. The coefficient of TUCE appears significant at a level of about 0.015, for example, while an incorrect inference drawn from the OLS results would have suggested TUCE to be insignificant. These WLS results can be used to draw the inferences sought. In particular, the t ratio for PSI is 3.69, which is highly significant, indicating that PSI does have a positive influence on the chance of earning an A even after controlling for ability and background. (Of course 32 observations are too few for strict reliance on the distributional properties of these WLS estimates, so the inferences drawn should be taken as tentative. As noted above, non-normality implies that the distributional properties hold only as an approximation in large samples. Thirty-two is not large enough for this approximation to be particularly tight.)

The coefficients can be interpreted as in regression with a continuous dependent variable except that they refer to the probability of a grade of A, rather than to the level of the grade itself. They can be used, for example, to predict the chances of earning an A. According to these results, a student with a grade point of 3.0, taught by traditional methods, and scoring 20 on the TUCE exam would earn an A with probability of .1286.

Three points are worthy of note. First, the reported $R^2$ of .7622, as obtained directly from the computer printout, is highly misleading. As explained above, it refers to the explained fraction of the variance of the transformed dependent variable (GRADE*W) and not to the original variable. Recomputation of the $R^2$ using the original variables yields the number .3755. Note that this value is smaller than the one reported above for the OLS analysis. By no means does this suggest that the OLS results are better. Rather it demonstrates the inappropriateness of the $R^2$ statistic in analyses involving qualitative variables.

Second, the sum of squared errors (SSE) has a useful interpretation beyond that in the standard regression model. The effect of the weighting is to divide each observation by an estimate of the standard deviation of the error term in that observation. Thus the weighted residual has a variance that is approximately 1, and the sum of squared residuals from the WLS analysis should behave approximately like a Chi-Square random variable with degrees of freedom N – K (32 – 4 = 28 in this case). Since a Chi-Square variable with degrees of freedom d has a mean of d and a variance of 2d, we can compute a statistic t = (SSE – (N – K))/ $\sqrt{(2(N-K))}$ which should behave like a drawing from Student's t distribution with $N - K$ degrees of freedom when $N - K$ is large. For the data used here we obtain $t = (22.74 - 28)/\text{sqrt}(56) = -.703$. Comparing this value to tabulated values of the t distribution, we conclude that it is not an unlikely outcome and therefore does not raise questions about the appropriateness of the model. Had it been larger than say 2.1, we might well reject the linear probability model as an adequate description of the data employed here.

Finally, while the results of this problem make the linear probability model appear quite acceptable, there are difficulties with it to be explained below.

### 1.2.3 A DIFFICULTY WITH GOLDBERGER'S PROCEDURE AND A SECOND EXAMPLE

One difficulty that arises with some frequency is that the estimates of $b_k$ in the first OLS regression lead to values of $\Sigma \hat{b}_k X_{ik}$ (or estimated values of the probability that $Y_i$ equals one) that are less than zero or greater than one.[8] This problem is not necessarily very severe. Given the LPM assumption (equation 1.6), the probability estimates are unbiased but will differ from the true value, being perhaps negative or greater than one simply due to sampling error. A practical solution is to truncate the estimates of $\Sigma \hat{b}_k X_{ik}$ to values close to zero or one, say .001 or .999.

If there are very many values that fall out of the range 0 to 1, especially if they do so by very much, then we might be led to wonder about the reasonableness of the assumption in equation 1.6. That is, we may be led to wonder whether or not our specification of the process as a linear probability model is in fact tenable. For example, Ostrom and Aldrich (1978), in an example that we will detail below, examined the relationship between the incidence of large-scale war and the number of major power nation states or alliances involving major powers in the international system from 1824 to 1938. The dependent variable was dichotomous, 1 if there was a large-scale war in a year, 0 if not. The independent variable was the number of major actors in the international system that year. Since several of the hypotheses were approximated by a linear probability model, Goldberger's estimation technique was used with an LPM of X linearly related to Y. The first stage OLS regression yielded 12% of the cases having a negative "probability" of war (all the years with a bipolar system; the estimated "probability" was about $-.07$), too high a percentage to attribute solely to "sampling error." The conclusion reached was that the assumption of the LPM, in combination with the assumed model, was implausible. Rather, a different set of assumptions was necessary.[9]

## 1.3 A Dichotomous Response Variable
## with Replicated Data

A random variable which can take on only two different values, designated as 1 and 0 for convenience, is known in statistics as a "Bernoulli response variable" and has associated with it a parameter, say P, that represents the probability of observing a response Y = 1. A single observation, say $Y_i$, on the dichotomous dependent variable of the previous section is an example of a Bernoulli random variable. In equation 1.6 we specified that the probability of a positive response, designated there as $P(Y_i = 1)$, depended on the values of K independent variables, that is,

$$P_i = P(Y_i = 1) = \Sigma b_k X_{ix}$$

Since the $X_{ik}$ are presumed to vary across observations, the parameter $P_i$ also changes, so we would say that each $Y_i$ follows a different Bernoulli distribution. Thus in section 1.3, a sample of size N represented drawings from N different Bernoulli distributions. The sum of N independent drawings (or N replications) from the same Bernoulli distribution (that is with the same probability, P, of success) is known as a "binomial response variable" and has associated with it two parameters, N and P.

Binomial variables also arise in social science contexts. In particular, it is not uncommon to encounter data sets in which observations can be grouped into subsets with the independent variables taking on the same values across all observations within a group. For example, in the Ostrom-Aldrich example in the last section, there were 111 data points. However, there were only five different values to the single independent variable. There were 13 cases of two major actors in the international system, 17 of three, 54 of four, 11 of five, and 16 of six actors. Since the only variable assumed relevant in that model was the number of major actors, the probability of war is the same for all years with the same number of actors. We could (and implicitly do) treat all 54 years with four major actors as drawings, or replications, from the same distribution, and the total number of wars begun during years with four actors as a binomial variable.

More generally, let the number of groups in a data set be designated by M (in Ostrom-Aldrich, M = 5) and let $N_j$, $(j = 1, \ldots, M)$ represent the number of observations within a group, (in Ostrom-Aldrich, $N_1 = 13$,

$N_2 = 17$, $N_3 = 54$, $N_4 = 11$, and $N_5 = 16$). Identify the $N_j$ distinct observations on Y within group j as $Y_{ij}$, $(i = 1, \ldots, N_j)$, and define

$$Y_j = \overset{N_j}{\Sigma} Y_{ij}.$$

The groups are defined so that each exogenous variable is constant across the $N_j$ observations in a group; designate these constant values as $X_{jk}$, $(k = 1, \ldots K)$. Since the probability of a positive response depends only on the $X_k$ and parameters $b_k$, it too is constant across observations in a group. That is

$$P(Y_{ij} = 1) = P_j = \Sigma b_k X_{jk}$$

for all $i = 1, \ldots, N_j$, $j = 1, \ldots, M$. Clearly the $Y_{ij}$'s are Bernoulli variables with parameter $P_j$, and $Y_j$, defined above, is binomial with parameters $P_j$ and $N_j$ (so long as the $N_j$ observations $Y_{ij}$ in group j are independent). From a theoretical point of view it matters little whether we treat as the focus of our analysis the binomial observations $Y_j$, $(j = 1, \ldots, M)$, or the Bernoulli observations $Y_{ij}$, $(i = 1, \ldots, N_j, j = 1, \ldots, M)$, since the information content is the same in either set. But from a practical point of view, the binomial variables represent a much smaller set of numbers (M) than do the binomial variables (N, where $N = \overset{M}{\Sigma} N_j$). So it generally proves more economical to treat the binomial (or "grouped," or "replicated") responses $Y_j$ as the unit of analysis.

What appears to be an advantage for binomial variables turns out to be only illusory. Define the fraction of positive responses within group j as $f_j = Y_j / N_j$. (The sample proportion $f_j$ is an estimate of $P_j$, the population proportion.) While the Bernoulli variable $Y_i$ of section 1.2 was limited to two values (0 or 1), the group proportion $f_j$ can assume $N_j + 1$ different values $(0/N_j, 1/N_j, \ldots, N_j/N_j)$. It would seem that if we regress $f_j$ on the independent variables, then the difficulties encountered in section 1.2 would not be so severe. That is, under the linear probability model assumption, $E(f_j) = P_i = \Sigma b_k X_{jk}$, so we can write the regression equation

$$f_j = \Sigma b_k X_{jk} + u_j \qquad [1.10]$$

Since $f_j$ is a closer approximation to a continuous dependent variable, it would seem that OLS regression of $f_j$ on $X_{jk}$ would suffice. However, little is changed from section 1.2. OLS regression would continue to yield unbiased estimates, given assumption 1.6. But as before, the assumption of homoscedasticity would fail, as the variance of $u_j$ would depend on the $b_k$ and $X_{jk}$ values.[10] Therefore, a weighted least squares procedure, similar to Goldberger's as presented above, is more appropriate. A one-step procedure is all that is required in this case. In section 1.2, the first OLS regression was used to estimate the weights, $w_i$. Here, we can use the observed frequencies or proportions $f_j$ themselves to compute the weights:

$$w_j = [N_j / [(f_j)(1 - f_j)]]^{1/2} \qquad [1.11]$$

The weights can then be used as in the Goldberger procedure. In sum, the grouped or replicated data allow us (only) the shortcut of estimating $w_j$ from the original data without recourse to the first OLS regression. Otherwise, this binomial variable case is the same as the Bernoulli case.[11]

The final similarity to the last section is that statistical properties of the estimates hold only as large sample approximations, though here we might obtain them from the fact that normality of $u_j$ holds as a reasonable approximation for a large number of observations in each group. The only real difference in this regard is that with replicated or binomial data, "large samples" refers to a large number of replications, $N_j$, for each observation, not to a large number of groups or observations, M.

### 1.4 Polytomous or Multiple Category Dependent Variables

So far, we have examined only the dichotomous variable. This is a special case of the more general problem of categorical dependent variables.[12] Party identification, for example, is usually a nominal or categorical variable. Choice of travel (say, car, bus, or subway), occupation, religion, and many other variables in the social sciences may be *in principle* nominal, while practical measurement problems may yield only nominal measures of many others. Let us consider the case of J mutually exclusive and exhaustive categories, which can be labeled arbitrarily as $1, 2, \ldots, J$, but the numberings can not be taken to indicate order, let alone magnitude.

An obvious approach would be to divide the dependent variable, $Y_i$, into a set of dichotomous variables. If there are J categories, there will be J such variables, say $Y_{ij}$, which equal one if $Y_i$ equals j, zero otherwise. For party identification, for example, there are three categories, Republican, Independent, and Democrat (assuming them only categorical, not ordinal). Thus, we will have three dichotomous dependent variables, say $Y_{i1}$, $Y_{i2}$, and $Y_{i3}$, respectively. Then $Y_{i1}$ will be one if individual i is identified as a Republican, zero if i is not a Republican, and so on.

Since each $Y_{ij}$ is a dichotomous, or Bernoulli, variable, we could assume that each one of the $Y_{ij}$'s may be modeled as a linear probability model:

$$Y_{ij} = \Sigma b_{kj} X_{ik} + u_{ij} \qquad j = 1, 2, \ldots, J \qquad [1.12]$$

The only difference between equations 1.12 and the LPM of section 1.2 is that 1.12 includes J equations instead of just one. Further, if the assumptions analogous to 1.6 can be assumed to hold for all J of the equations, the analysis of section 1.2 applies directly to each of the J equations separately. That is, OLS estimates of each separate equation in 1.12 will be unbiased but the variance of $u_i$ will again be heteroscedastic.

There is one conceivable problem. We are estimating probabilities. In section 1.2, we faced the problem that the estimated probability that $Y_i$ equalled 1 might be negative or greater than 1. Here, we face the additional problem that the probabilities estimated for each observation must sum to 1 across all equations. For example, the probability that individual i is a Republican, a Democrat, or an Independent must be 1. And, it is not particularly obvious that estimating three, four, or even more equations separately will yield the appropriate sum. By algebraic manipulation of the so-called "normal equations" of regression (Johnston, 1984) it turns out that least squares estimation of each equation separately will automatically meet that condition—provided that each equation in 1.12 contains an intercept term. This fact yields an added bonus. There is no reason to estimate all J equations. Rather, we need only estimate J – 1 of them, for the unestimated equation can be solved for algebraically. And so doing will yield the same answer that you would get from running the regression of it. To see why, suppose that everyone is either a Republican or a Democrat. This variable is a dichotomous one, just as we studied in section 1.2. But, we could have, as in this section, constructed two dichotomous variables, one for Republican (say $Y_{i1}$) and one for Democratic ($Y_{i2}$) identification. And, we could run regressions on both of these, just as we have suggested doing here. But we don't have to, for the coefficients in estimating, say $Y_{i2}$, would be equal to the negative of their counterparts in $Y_{i1}$. (The intercept for $Y_{i2}$ would be one minus the intercept of $Y_{i1}$.) And, that is, in effect, just what we would do in solving for $P(Y_i = 0)$ in the dichotomous case: knowing $P(Y_i = 1)$ means that solving for $P(Y_i = 0)$ is straightforward, being $1 - P(Y_i = 1)$.

So, in short, the extension to the polytomous case is straightforward so far. The OLS estimates of each of the J (or J – 1) equations in 1.12 will be unbiased. The disturbance terms, $u_{ij}$, will be heteroscedastic as before. Again, a weighted, two-step approach could be used.[13] However, in Goldberger's procedure, the intercept is dropped from the equations, being replaced by the weight, $w_i$. What this means is that the estimated probabilities might *not* sum to 1 after the second round of estimation. Beyond that, however, the extension of the Goldberger procedure is rather straightforward. It is not used very often, however, since a procedure to be discussed in Chapter 3 is more attractive.

Everything we have considered from section 1.2 to this point rests on the linear probability assumption. We have suggested that assumption is problematic. It is time to consider why it is so.

### 1.5 The Linearity Assumption

Throughout the last three sections, we have argued that, so long as the linearity assumption of equation 1.6 is maintained, least squares estimation with a correction for heteroscedasticity and some care in interpretation in small samples is viable. Here, we argue that, since $\Sigma b_k X_{ik}$ must be interpreted as a probability, the fact that it is linear in X makes it highly suspect.

Probabilities are, of course, restricted to the interval from 0 to 1. As a result, the linear probability model imposes harsh and quite possibly arbitrary constraints on the values that the regression coefficients $b_k$ may assume. Suppose we have a bivariate case:

$$P(Y_i = 1) = E(Y_i) = b_0 + b_1 X_i$$

and suppose that $b_1$ is positive. Then, the smallest value that $X_i$ takes on, say $X_{(1)}$, must yield a predicted probability that is greater than or equal to zero. The largest value of $X_i$, say $X_{(N)}$, must yield a probability no larger than one:

$$0 \leq b_0 + b_1 X_{(1)} < b_0 + b_1 X_{(N)} \leq 1$$

These constraints are dictated by the nature of the linear probability model. (Of course $X_{(1)}$ and $X_{(N)}$ should be interchanged for negative $b_1$.)

The above constraints may not be terribly bothersome. For example, $Y_i$ might be a Republican or a Democratic vote (say $Y_i$ equals 0 and 1, respectively), while $X_i$ might be the party i identifies with (say, $X_i$ equals 1 if Democratic identifier, 0 if Republican, ignoring independents or other party affiliations). Then, $b_0$ will be the probability that a Republican votes for the Democratic candidate and $b_0 + b_1$ is the probability of a Democratic supporting his or her own party's candidate. In this case, the constraints that $0 \leq b_0 < (b_0 + b_1) \leq 1$ pose no difficulty.

Suppose instead that X is the differential evaluation of the two candidates. The SRC/CPS National Election Studies regularly ask people to rank each candidate on a 0 to 100 scale. The difference between the two has been shown to be very strongly related to the candidate supported (Abramson et al., 1983 and sources cited therein). This X variable runs from –100 (ranking the Republican at 100, the Democrat at 0, for example) to +100 (a 0 for the Republican, 100 for the Democrat). The constraints then require that

$$0 \leq b_0 + b_1(X = -100) \quad \text{or} \quad 0 \leq b_0 - 100b_1$$

$$b_0 + b_1(X = +100) \leq 1 \quad \text{or} \quad b_0 + 100b_1 \leq 1$$

Suppose the constraints are exact (i.e., $b_0 - 100 b_1 = 0$; $b_0 + 100 b_1 = 1$). This represents the most generous constraint. Then, if we add the two together, we get that $2b_0 = 1$ or $b_0 = .5$. Solving for $b_1$ yields a value of .005. In other words, for every unit increase in a relative liking of the Democrat compared to the Republican, the probability of voting Democrat can increase by no more than .005, and we know this even before we do any estimation—or even data gathering!

Consider a third example in which $Y_i$ represents home ownership (1 if yes and 0 if no) and $X_i$ represents family wealth, say in thousands of dollars. In this case $b_0$ is the probability that a family with zero wealth will own, and $b_1$ is the change in probability of owning resulting from a one thousand dollar increase in family wealth. Assuming maximum and minimum values for family wealth is a bit troublesome to begin with, but suppose those values are 1000 and –10. Then, assuming the effect of wealth on ownership is positive, we find that $b_1$ is at most $1/1010$ and that $10b_1 \leq b_0 \leq 1 - 1000b_1$. Thus the linearity assumption implies that the difference in the probability of ownership between families with net wealths of zero and $100,000 is at most 0.09901. That must be viewed as a disturbing implication of the linearity assumption. And note that it derives from conservative assumptions about the potential range in family wealth. Allowing X to be as large as 100,000 would require that same probability difference to be smaller than .001!

The first and last examples above represent extreme cases; both get worse as additional exogenous variables are added to the right-hand side. The two points to be noted with regard to the restrictions are that the assumption of a linear model *inherently* imposes constraints on the marginal effects of exogenous variables (i.e., the effect on Y of a one unit change in X) and that those constraints are not taken into account by least squares estimation.

A second objection to the linear specification is that the marginal effect of exogenous variables is constant. In the home ownership example, for instance, the model posits that an increase in wealth of $50,000 will have the same effect on ownership regardless of whether the family starts with zero wealth or wealth of one million. Certainly, a family with $50,000 wealth is more likely to own a home than one with zero wealth. But, a millionaire is very likely to own a home, and the addition of $50,000 is not going to increase the likelihood of home ownership by very much. Similarly, an increase in wealth from $0 to $1,000 is not going to increase the likelihood of house ownership much; it will be *very* near zero in both cases. A specification with more initiative appeal would express $Pr(Y_i = 1)$ as a nonlinear function of $X_i$, one which approaches zero at slower and slower rates as $X_i$ gets small and approaches one at slower and slower rates as $X_1$ gets very large. Such a specification is suggested in Figure 1 below as the solid sigmoid or S-shaped curve. It should be contrasted with the linear specification represented by the broken line. Note that, as drawn, the linear specification is not consistent with any values of X greater than $X_0$, for the "probability" that $Y_i$ equals one exceeds certainty beginning at that point. If we had observations up to $X_1$ or beyond, we would force the straight line to be flatter; that is, to force a smaller magnitude on $b_1$, strictly because of the constraint that $Pr(Y_i = 1)$ can not exceed one.

Even with a continuous dependent variable, the linear regression model is generally taken only as an approximation. If we suspect a priori or if the data suggest a nonlinear relationship between Y and X, then we abandon the linear model in favor of a nonlinear one, say by introducing polynomials in X (as done in Ostrom and Aldrich, 1978, for example) or taking logarithms. A priori there is every reason to suspect that the expectation of a qualitative variable as a function of X must be nonlinear in X. Since that expectation must fall between 0 and 1, it makes little sense to choose a functional form which satisfies this constraint only by the imposition of artificial constraints on the range of values the regression coefficients may assume.

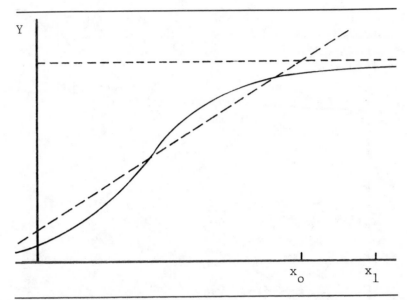

Figure 1.   Sigmoid Versus Linear Specifications

## 1.6  The Effect of an Incorrect Linearity Assumption

Suppose that the true relationship between Y and X, or, more correctly, between the expected value of Y and X, is nonlinear, but in our ignorance of the "true" relationship we adopt the linear probability model as an approximation. What can be said about estimates and inferences drawn from least squares and weighted least squares?

The only positive statement is that the OLS and weighted least squares estimates will tend to indicate the correct sign of the effect of X on Y. But none of the distributional properties holds, so statistical inferences will have no statistical justification. To see this, recall that all of the distributional properties of the least squares estimator as noted in section 1.1 depend crucially on the assumption $E(Y|X) = \Sigma b_k X_{ki}$. If that assumption fails, the estimates will not be unbiased and their variance will not be correctly estimated. Furthermore, use of the normal distribution to construct confidence intervals and test hypotheses is totally unwarranted even in large samples since implied variance estimates are biased. Thus when a least squares coefficient estimate is positive, for example, we have no way of determining the probability that the positive estimate was due only to chance.

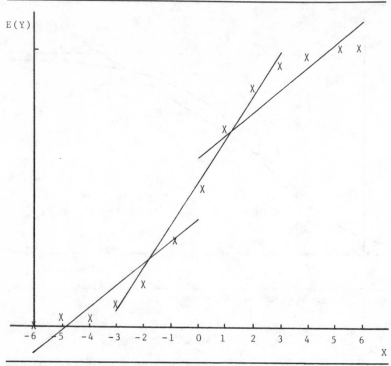

**Figure 2.** Linear Approximations to a Nonlinear Model

Second, estimates will at best approximate the true relationship only within the range of the data in the sample. Consider the relationship between Y and a single exogenous variable as depicted in Figure 2. (The points marked with an X may be thought of as values of the true $P(Y = 1)$ for dichotomous relationship of section 1.2 or as values $f_j$ for large $N_j$ in the replicated data case of section 1.3.) Clearly the relationship between $E(Y)$ and X is nonlinear. If we attempt to approximate this relationship by least squares regression, the estimates we obtain will be highly sensitive to the range of data included in the sample. If we use only the data corresponding to values of X between −3 and +3 inclusively, the OLS estimates on average will be $E(Y) = .5 + .1554X$. If the sample contains data corresponding only to values of X from −6 to 0, the estimates would be $E(Y) = .3875 + .0787X$, and if the range were from 0 to +6, the estimates would be $E(Y) = .6125 + .0787X$. These lines are plotted in Figure 2. In each case the least squares fit is reasonably good only within the range of the sample. Clearly extrapolations outside this range are invalid.

Next, note the probability estimates outside the range of 0 to 1 do not occur only by chance. Indeed two of the equations above yield probability estimates which are either negative or greater than 1 even within the range of the data. And these numbers reported above represent limiting values for very large samples. Estimates based on smaller samples could be much worse. The result is due to the linear approximation and not just chance occurrence.

Even when qualitatively correct, least squares estimates may seriously misstate the marginal effect of X on Y. In Figure 2, for example, that marginal effect is as high as .2 but the closest estimate was .15 and two of the estimates were .0787. As a more extreme case, suppose the true relationship could be represented by a step function—whenever X is below some critical value $X_c$, Y assumes the value 0 while Y is 1 whenever $X \geq X_c$. This relationship between Y and X is a perfect one, in the sense that X explains Y exactly. But in fact least squares would never detect such a perfect fit, and, if the range on X in the sample was very wide, the estimated marginal effect would be quite small, approaching zero. Relatedly, the $R^2$ measure is of limited use when the dependent variable is dichotomous. In the standard regression model an $R^2$ of 1 indicates a perfect fit—the dependent variable is explained exactly by the regression equation. But, when Y can assume only two values, such a perfect fit is essentially impossible. The maximum value of $R^2$ is generally less than 1 and, moreover, will vary from sample to sample depending on the values of X in the sample, even if the true model remains the same.

Finally, many of the steps suggested in regression analysis for improving the quality of least squares estimates may in fact have adverse effects on those estimates in the qualitative variable case. In regression analysis with correct specification, increasing the variance of X in the sample has the positive effect of making the estimates more precise. But increasing the range of X in the qualitative variable case tends to decrease the estimates of the regression coefficients themselves. While the variance estimates will decline, they are invalid. As noted, the linear probability model necessarily implies heteroscedastic disturbances. In order to obtain more efficient estimates and to derive distributional properties, the suggestion was to use weighted least squares, using equations 1.8 or 1.11 to compute the weights. Both of these involve terms of the form $1/(P(1-P))$. The weights are largest when P is near 0 or 1, and smallest when P is near .5. That means observations at the extremes will receive more weight than those near the center. If the true relation is nonlinear, those extreme values will be the worst fit, exacerbating the problems noted above. Thus we see that increasing the variance in X and correcting for heteroscedasticity, commendable practices when the specification is correct, actually make things worse.

To summarize the results of this section, the incorrect assumption of linearity will lead to least squares estimates which (1) have no known distributional properties, (2) are sensitive to the range of the data, (3) may grossly understate the magnitude of the true effects, (4) systematically yield probability predictions outside the range of 0 to 1, and (5) get worse as standard statistical practices for improving the estimates are employed. Of course the criticisms noted above are not unique to linear specifications. If the true relationship is linear but we assume a nonlinear model, the same problems arise in reverse. We should choose that specification that seems most appropriate. In specifying a model for probabilities that must lie in the 0-1 interval, choosing a form like the linear that is not similarly constrained is not appropriate.

## 2. SPECIFICATION OF NONLINEAR PROBABILITY MODELS

### 2.0 Introduction

The thrust of the last chapter is that there are a variety of reasons why the assumption that a probability model is linear in the independent variables is unrealistic in most cases. Further, if we incorrectly specify the model as linear, the statistical properties derived under the linearity assumption will not, in general, hold. (Indeed, the parameters being estimated may not even be relevant.) The obvious solution to this problem is to specify a nonlinear probability model in place of the linear probabililty model, and this chapter will example a variety of possible nonlinear models. The first section of this chapter discusses specification as a general problem. The second section examines specific models for the cases of dichotomous dependent variables with either grouped (replicated or binomial) data or ungrouped (Bernoulli) data. The third section describes a model of behavior from which various nonlinear specifications may be derived. The fourth section discusses the more difficult case of polytomous dependent variables (i.e., ones with more than two nominal categories). The last two sections examine the proposed functional forms in detail.

### 2.1 The General Problem of Specification

Statistical inference begins by assuming that the model to be estimated and used for making inferences is correctly specified. The presumption is that the substantive theory of concern gives rise to and justifies the particular statistical model. It is easy enough to show that incorrect model specification has truly substantial implications, as all statistical properties of the estimates may be destroyed. To put it bluntly, incorrect model specification leads to the wrong answers. There are two different aspects of specification.[14] The more commonly mentioned aspect concerns specifying the correct set of variables to be included in the model, i.e., that the mean of Y is a function of only the K included variables:

$$E(Y_i) = f(X_{i1}, \ldots, X_{iK}) \qquad [2.1]$$

The second aspect is that the function happens to be linear:

$$E(Y_i) = f(X_{i1}, \ldots, X_{iK}) = \Sigma b_k X_{ik} \qquad [2.2]$$

Why is the linear specification so popular? There are two basic (and related) reasons. On practical grounds, linear models are mathematically simple, so that statisticians have been able to learn a lot about them, and computer programs have been written to do the estimation. On theoretical grounds, the simplicity leads to their adoption, justified by a version of Occam's Razor: In the absence of any theoretical guidance to the contrary, begin by assuming the simplest case.

The difficulty with the linear probability model is that there are often reasons to believe that it is not tenable. Thus, Occam's Razor, by implication, would say: With some theoretical guidance to the contrary, do *not* assume the simplest case. There remain, of course, the practical grounds for the linearity specification. Fortunately, at least some nonlinear specifications are tractable and only a little more difficult, expensive, and limited than linear models.

## 2.2 Alternative Nonlinear Functional Forms for the Dichotomous Case

The problem with the linear probability model specification is that $\Sigma b_k X_{ik}$ is used to approximate a probability number, $P_i [P_i \equiv P(Y_i = 1)]$, constrained to be from 0 to 1, while $\Sigma b_k X_{ik}$ is not so constrained. One way of approaching this problem is to transform $P_i$ to eliminate one or both constraints. For the dichotomous case, we can eliminate the upper bound, $P_i = 1$, by looking at the ratio $P_i/(1 - P_i)$. This ratio must be positive (since $0 < P_i < 1$), but there is no upper bound.[15] As $P_i$ approaches one, $P_i/(1 - P_i)$ goes toward infinity. We can eliminate the lower boundary of zero by taking the natural logarithm, $\log[P_i/(1 - P_i)]$

the result of which can be any real number from negative to positive infinity. We can now (arbitrarily) assume that this transformed dependent variable is a linear function of X:

$$\log [P_i/(1 - P_i)] = \Sigma b_k X_{ik} \equiv Z_i \qquad [2.3]$$

(Since we will be writing $\Sigma b_k X_{ik}$ repeatedly in this chapter, we will use $Z_i$ to stand for that summation.)

What we want is an expression for $P_i$. The solution can be obtained by using antilogarithms and algebraic manipulation. The natural logarithm has a base number of e, an irrational number, where $\log (e^x) = x$, and thus, the antilog of x is $e^x$. The more common notation is "exp($\cdot$)" which means e raised to the power of whatever is inside the parentheses. Thus, the solution of equation 2.3 for $P_i$ is

$$P_i = \exp(Z_i)/(1 + \exp(Z_i)) \qquad [2.4]$$

This expression, commonly referred to as the "logistic function," is continuous and can take on any value from 0 to 1. It is near 0 when $Z_i$ is near negative infinity, it increases monotonically with $Z_i$, and it goes to 1 as $Z_i$ goes to positive infinity. It is, in fact, a smooth S-shaped curve as depicted in Figure 1, Chapter 1, which is symmetric about the point $Z_i = 0$. Unlike the linear specification, it satisfies the 0-1 constraint on $P_i$ *without* also constraining $Z_i$ ($\Sigma b_k X_{ik}$).

These characteristics of the function described in equation 2.4 make it an attractive alternative to the linear probability model for dichotomous dependent variables. It may be reasonable enough, but why this one? Why not others? It is, after all, as arbitrary as picking linearity. In fact, there are an infinite number of alternatives to equation 2.4, and, as with equation 2.4, some of these have been developed as alternative models for estimation. Seven of these are depicted in Figure 3, and we shall describe them briefly to provide an indication of the wide "menu" of choices available.

The first of these seven, in Figure 3.A, is called the "truncated linear probability model." This model assumes something quite like the linear probability model. It is a constant, linear function, but only over a range of values of $Z_i$ (and, hence, $X_{ik}$). At some low of value of $Z_i$ the truncated LPM reaches 0 and is assumed to be exactly 0 from there on down to negative infinity. At some higher value, the probability of $Y_i$ equals 1 and remains so through positive infinity.[16] This model is an obvious variation of the original LPM and does not impose any arbitrary constraints on the coefficients in $\Sigma b_k X_{ik}$. It does constrain the

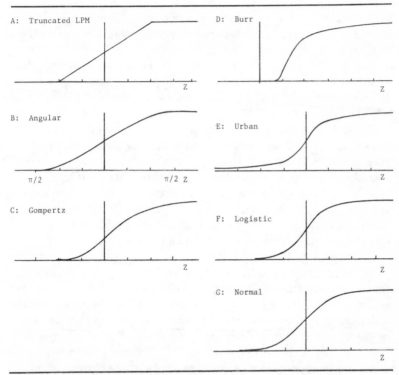

**Figure 3.    Graphs of Alternative Specifications**

relationship between the $X_{ik}$'s and $Y_i$, however, at extreme values of the $X_{ik}$. In particular, it imposes the constraint that changes in $Z_i$ have *no* effect on $P_i$ at high and at low ranges of $Z_i$. Further, estimation requires a linear programming approach that is more cumbersome and costly than OLS.

Figure 3.B illustrates what is known as the "angular transformation." This model is like the above in that, below some value of $Z_i$, $P_i$ is 0 and that, above some $Z_i$ value, $P_i$ is 1. In the range in which $P_i$ varies as $Z_i$ does, we no longer have a straight line, but rather a curve that smoothly approaches and touches the two constraints.[17] The rigidity of the extreme value constraints is an unappealing here as before.

The "Gompertz curve" is depicted in Figure 3C.[18] This curve has no constraints, unlike the two models above and the original LPM. In fact, it only gets very close to, but never reaches, 0 and 1; such a curve is said to "asymptotically approach 0 from above and 1 from below." It is not a symmetric curve, since it approaches 0 on the left more rapidly than it approaches 1 on the right. Therefore, it is most plausible only when there is some a priori reason to expect asymmetry. Otherwise, symmetry is simpler and can be justified as an assumption by recourse to the logic of Occam's Razor.

The fourth example, in Figure 3D, is associated with the "Burr distribution." It requires that $Z_i$ be strictly positive, a requirement that arises in practice from time to time. Otherwise, the curve is smooth and imposes no upper bound.[19]

The last three curves have many similarities. "Urban's Curve,"[20] the logistic curve, and the normal curve are all sigmoid curves that are symmetric about a $Z_i$ of 0 and impose no constraints on $Z_i$. The only essential difference lies in the thickness of the tails of the curves, i.e., how rapidly or slowly the curves approach 0 and 1. Urban's curve has the thickest tails (i.e., approaches extreme values must slowly), but the difference is likely to be relatively small and observable only with many observations at extreme values of $X_{ik}$, and thus $Z_i$.

The logistic and normal curves are so similar as to yield essentially identical results. In practice they yield estimated choice probabilities that differ by less than .02 and which can be distinguished, in the sense of statistical significance, only with very large samples. The choice between them, therefore, revolves around practical concerns such as the availability and flexibility of computer programs and personal preference and experience. These two have received the most attention by researchers (and computer programmers). That is, they are better developed than the other examples, are much more widely used, and are available in computer programs much more commonly. Their importance is such that we will focus most of our attention on them. The equation for the logistic curve is

$$\text{logistic:} \quad F(Z) = \exp(Z)/(1 + \exp(Z)) \qquad [2.5]$$

where exp, recall, represents the irrational number e (the base of natural logarithms) raised to the power of whatever is in the parentheses (here, Z). Also note that, taking $P_i = F(Z_i)$, equation 2.5 is the same as equation 2.4. Thus, the example in the beginning of this chapter is of the logistic curve. The normal curve is, technically, the cumulative normal distribution function, which is so commonly employed in statistics:

$$\text{normal:} \quad F(Z) = \int_{-\infty}^{Z} \frac{1}{\sqrt{2\pi}} \, \exp(-u^2/2)du \equiv \Phi(Z) \qquad [2.6]$$

Since the equation is cumbersome to write, $\Phi(Z)$ is often used to denote the cumulative normal.

At this point, then, we have a fairly wide "menu" of alternatives. In practice, the nonlinear specification problem is solved in most cases by picking either the logistic or normal curve (and there is little to guide the choice between the two). But, the choice of specification remains fairly arbitrary. In the next section we will review some work that provides a theoretical rationale.

## 2.3 Derivation of Nonlinear Transformations from a Behavioral Model

The logic of this section is based on a formal, rational choice perspective on behavior as advanced by Luce and Suppes (1965) and others and placed in an econometric framework by McFadden (1973). It is important to point out that this rationale is sufficient to justify the use of these curves, but it is not necessary. That is, one may still employ these nonlinear specifications without assuming that they arise from the choice theory described here.

In the behavioral sciences, $Y_i$ is often an observation on the behavior of an individual, agency, or group. And it is often the case that the agent, say an individual, is faced with a choice of selecting between two alternatives. The rational choice approach asserts that the agent has preferences over these two alternatives, and that the agent will choose the more (most) preferred alternative. Thus, we might let $W_{i1}$ denote agent i's preference for alternative one and $W_{i2}$ i's preference for alternative two.[21] The central presumption, then, would be that i would choose alternative one over two if $W_{i1} > W_{i2}$ and choose two over if $W_{i1} < W_{i2}$.

To model this process, preference may be assumed to be a linear function of exogenous variables, say:

$$W_{i1} = \Sigma a_{k1} X_{ik} + v_{i1} \qquad \text{and}$$

$$W_{i2} = \Sigma a_{k2} X_{ik} + v_{i2} \qquad [2.7]$$

The $v_i$'s are taken to be unmeasured factors, approximation errors, and/or random aspects of behavior. Then, $W_{i1}$ will be greater than $W_{i2}$ if $W_{i1} - W_{i2} > 0$ and it will be less than $W_{i2}$ if $W_{i1} - W_{i2} < 0$. Suppose we let $Y_i^*$ be this difference, then:

$$Y_i^* \equiv W_{i1} - W_{i2} = \Sigma(a_{k1} - a_{k2}) X_{ik} + (v_{i1} - v_{i2}) \qquad [2.8a]$$

We can simplify equation 2.8a by letting $b_k = (a_{k1} - a_{k2})$ and $u_i = (v_{i2} - v_{i1})$, obtaining:[22]

$$Y_i^* = \Sigma b_k X_{ik} - u_i \qquad [2.8b]$$

Often, the $W_i$ terms are not discussed, and one starts with equation 2.8b as the primitive description of preference.

The choice perspective says that agent i chooses alternative one over alternative two if $W_{i1} > W_{i2}$, or if $Y_i^* > 0$. But, by equation 2.8b, this means that alternative one is chosen if $\Sigma b_k X_{ik} - u_i > 0$, i.e., if $u_i < \Sigma b_k X_{ik}$. If $Y_i$, the observed choice made by agent i, is equal to one when $Y_i^* > 0$ (i.e., alternative one is chosen) and is equal to zero when $Y_i^* < 0$ (or alternative two is chosen), then we are led naturally to a probabilistic statement:

$$P(Y_i = 1) = P(Y_i^* > 0) = P(u_i < \Sigma b_k X_{ik}) \qquad [2.9]$$

So, to know or estimate $P(Y_i = 1)$, we need to know the total (or cumulative) probability that $u_i$ is less than $\Sigma b_k X_{ik}$, and this requires knowledge of the probability distribution of $u_i$. If $u_i$ is a continuous random variable, as seems most reasonable, then (equation 2.9) can be written as:

$$P(u_i < \Sigma b_k X_{ik}) \equiv P(u_i < Z_i) = F(Z_i) = \int_{-\infty}^{Z_i} f(u)\,du \qquad [2.10]$$

where $F(\cdot)$ is the cumulative distribution function and $f(\cdot)$ is the probability density function of the random variable $u_i$ and again we simplify notation by defining $Z_i = \Sigma b_k X_{ik}$.

The last step, then, is to specify the probability distribution of $u_i$. If we assume that it follows a logistic distribution, we obtain the logistic curve (equation 2.5 and Figure 3f). If we assume that it follows the normal distribution, we obtain the normal curve specification (equation 2.6 and Figure 3g). In fact, there is some distribution function for $u_i$ that gives any of the nonlinear specifications $F(Z)$ such that $F(Z)$ is 0 at negative infinity, 1 at positive infinity and increases monotonically in between.[23]

What we have done, then, is provide a choice-based rationale for the dichotomous dependent variable, from which it is possible to derive a particular nonlinear specification of the probability model. All of the nonlinear probability models (as well as the LPM itself) are based on a linear relationship between the unobserved $Y_i^*$ and $X_{ik}$. We cannot observe (or, at least, measure) $Y_i^*$ as a continuous variable, measured at the interval level. Instead, we can measure the dichotomous $Y_i$, which is a function (in particular, a step function) of $Y^*$. $Y_i$ is related to $X_{ik}$, by the probability $P_i$, a transformation of $\Sigma b_k X_{ik}$. The choice of nonlinear specification is, in terms of the choice model here, dependent strictly upon the distribution of the disturbance term, $u_i$. To pick a particular nonlinear model is to pick implicitly a distribution of $u_i$. By the nature of the problem, we never know what the distribution is, yet we often assume that it is some particular one. And, the normal and logistic are two of the most commonly assumed distributions, providing still another rationale for their importance.

For a variety of reasons, therefore, the logistic and normal curve specifications are the two most commonly used alternatives to the linear specification of the probability model. These two models are called the "logit" and "probit" models, respectively. "Probit" is an abbreviation of the term "probability unit" (the term is attributed to C. R. Bliss) and was the first such model developed and studied (Finney, 1971). "Logit" stands for "logistic probability unit," so named by Berkson (1944). Other of the curves depicted above have similar names "Gompit," "Burrit," and so on. Since probit was the first developed, it acquired the nomenclature based on probability unit. Logit and so on are also probability units, so, some refer to probit as "normit" for "normal probability unit." Normit has not been as widely used, so we will follow common practice and refer to it as "probit."

## 2.4 Nonlinear Probability Specifications for Polytomous Variables

So far, we have considered only the case of a dichotomous $Y_i$. Both probit and logit, the nonlinear forms that we shall consider in detail, are applicable whether the data are grouped/replicated (i.e., binomial) or ungrouped (i.e., Bernoulli). Here we consider the case of there being more than two (say, J with $J > 2$) unordered, categorical values for $Y_i$, that is, the case of a polytomous $Y_i$.

In the last chapter, we extended the linear probability model to the polytomous dependent variable case by dividing the dependent variable $Y_i$ (where $Y_i$ takes on integer values from 1 to J) into J different dichotomous variables, $Y_{ij}$, where $Y_{ij}$ was one if outcome j was observed, zero if not. This led to the specification of J linear probability model equations:

$$P(Y_i = j) = P(Y_{ij} = 1) = \sum_{}^{K} b_{jk} X_{ik}$$

In the last two sections, we modified the linear equation by taking a nonlinear transformation of it, say $F(\Sigma b_k X_{ik})$. It would seem obvious to combine the two steps and specify J nonlinear probability model equations:

$$P(Y_i = j) = P(Y_{ij} = 1) = F\left(\overset{K}{\Sigma}b_{jk}X_{ik}\right)$$

Unfortunately, we can not ensure that the relevant probabilities will sum to one, and there are other problems that make this simple approach undesirable.

In place of the above, we shall follow an approach similar to that leading to equations 2.3 and 2.4 above (i.e., the logit model). First, take one of the equations, say the $J^{th}$ [i.e., $P(Y_i = J)$]. Then consider the odds that $Y_i$ equals one of the other outcomes, say j compared to J, and as before take the natural logarithms of those odds. This "log-odds ratio," then, is:

$$\log\,[P(Y_i = j)/P(Y_i = J)] = \overset{K}{\Sigma}b_{jk}X_{ik} \equiv Z_{ij} \text{ for } j \neq J = 1, \ldots, J-1 \quad [2.11]$$

Note the similarity to the dichotomous case. In equation 2.3, $P_i$ was $P(Y_i = 1)$, the numerator. The remaining outcome probability is $P(Y_i = 0)$, but in the dichotomous case, that is just $[1 - P(Y_i = 1)]$, the denominator. Then logs were taken, and that was set equal to $\Sigma b_k X_{ik}$ or $Z_i$. Here outcome J can be thought of as analogous to outcome zero in the dichotomous case, and equation 2.11 can be seen as similar to equation 2.3. The outcome J serves as a baseline for comparison of the other alternatives.

As in the dichotomous case, we can solve equation 2.11 for the probability that $Y_i$ equals outcome j:

$$P(Y_i = j) = [\exp(Z_{ij})]/[P(Y_i = J)] \quad \text{for } j = 1, \ldots, J-1 \quad [2.12]$$

This equation would be solvable if we knew $P(Y_i = J)$, and we can solve for that unknown because probabilities must sum to one ($\Sigma_j^J P(Y_i = j) = 1$). It turns out that $P(Y_i = J)$ is:

$$P(Y_i = J) = 1/\left[1 + \overset{J-1}{\underset{j=1}{\Sigma}} \exp(Z_{ij})\right] \quad [2.13]$$

Substitution into equation 2.12 yields expressions for the other probability terms:

$$P(Y_i = j) = [exp(Z_{ij})] / \left[ 1 + \sum_{j=1}^{J-1} exp(Z_{ij}) \right] \quad \text{for } j = 1, \ldots, J-1 \quad [2.14]$$

This specification, the "multinomial logit" model, is tractable, and is a generalization of the dichotomous dependent variable logit model.

We arbitrarily picked outcome J as our baseline; we could have picked any other outcome and obtained comparable results. Expressions 2.13 and 2.14 can be simplified into one expression if we add K zero parameters; $b_{Jk} = 0$ for $k = 1, \ldots, K$. Then 2.13 and 2.14 can be written as a single set of ratios:[24]

$$P(Y_i = j) = exp(\Sigma b_{jk} X_{ij})/D \quad \text{for all } j \ (j = 1, \ldots, J) \quad [2.15]$$

where

$$D = \sum_{j=1}^{J} [exp(\Sigma b_{jk} X_{ik})]$$

D, therefore, is just a normalizing denominator that weights the probability terms so that they do in fact add to one (and is, of course, the same as the denominator of equations 2.13 and 2.14). The numerator, therefore, is of more central concern, and it is analogous to the numerator of the dichotomous logit model, equations 2.4 and 2.5. All that 2.15 does is express 2.13 and 2.14 in one common form, it does not change the content of the expressions. The multinominal logit model is a rather straightforward extension of the dichotomous logit model, and adds no new assumptions.

It is reasonable to ask if the other six specifications, or even other possible models, might be extended to handle the polytomous dependent variable. Unfortunately, while there are, again, an infinite number of such forms, they turn out to be infeasible to estimate. (Multinomial probit, for example, involves probability expressions that are multiple integrals of the multivariate normal density. While accurate and simple approximations are available for the integral of the univariate density, comparable approximations are feasible for the multivariate integrals only up to about the fourth order. Beyond this dimension, computation is impractical.) In other words, multinomial probit, Gompit, and the like, are logically possible but impractical. Therefore, multinomial logit is the standard method for estimating unordered, multi-category dependent variables.[25]

While multinomial logit has become the standard model, it was derived in an ad hoc fashion. It is possible, however, to derive multinominal logit from a direct extension of the choice model presented in section 2.3. If $W_{ij}$ represents the unobserved, interval measure of preference by agent i for alternative j, then we assume that the observed variable is that agent i chooses alternative j (say, $Y_i = j$) if and only if $W_{ij}$ is the most preferred alternative (i.e., $W_{ij} > W_{ip}$ for all $p \neq j$). In other words, agent i chooses the most preferred alternative. We are then led to consider the expression:

$$P(Y_i = j) = P(W_{ij} > W_{ip} \quad \text{for all } p \neq j)$$

As before, we assume that $W_{ij}$ is a linear combination of the K independent variables $X_{ik}$, plus a disturbance term (in notation similar to that in the last section, $W_{ij} = \Sigma a_{jk} X_{ik} + v_{ij}$). As before, we would take the differences, and derive an expression for $P(Y_i = j)$ that is a function of the $X_{ik}$'s. The form of this function depends on the distribution of the disturbance terms. Unfortunately, all the obvious choices of a probabililty distribution, such as the normal and logistic distribution, are computationally impractical. McFadden (1974) showed that the multinomial logit model can be derived by assuming that the disturbances are distributed according to what is known as the independent "type I extreme value distribution." The difficulty, of course, is that there is no obvious rationale for assuming this particular distribution as there is for, say, the normal or logistic. Still, this rather ad hoc distributional assumption does provide a choice-based derivation of a tractable statistical model which has proven to be highly effective.

## 2.5 Behavior of the Logit and Probit Specifications

In the previous two sections, the probit and logit forms were suggested as alternatives to the linear probability model for qualitative dependent variables. Effective use of probit and logit analysis will require a thorough understanding of these functional forms for choice probabilities. In the linear regression model,

$$Y_i = \Sigma b_k X_{ik} = u_i \qquad [2.16]$$

$b_k$ is interpreted as the amount by which $Y_i$ will change, on average and other things equal, when $X_{ik}$ increases by one unit. We seek here the analogous interpretation for logit and probit models.

Recall first that the structural derivation of logit and probit forms in sections 2.3 and 2.4 contained relations such as

$$Y_i^* = \Sigma b_k X_{ik} + u_i \qquad [2.17]$$

where $Y^*$ represents the latent (unobservable) preference for an alternative. This equation is exactly analogous to the regression equation, and the interpretation of all components is the same. But $b_k$ measures the effect of a change in $X_{ik}$ on the continuous and unobserved variable $Y_i^*$, not the discrete observed variable $Y_i$. Also, since $Y_i^*$ is never directly observed, its scale cannot be determined. That is, equation 2.17 could be multiplied by an arbitrary positive constant without changing the sign of $Y_i^*$. And such a change would have no effect whatsoever on the observed qualitative outcomes $Y_i$, since the latter measures only the sign, not the magnitude, of $Y_i^*$. Thus both probit and logit employ normalizations to fix the otherwise arbitrary scales. In probit, the convenient normalization is one that fixes the standard deviation $u_i$ at one, and in logit the normalization fixes the standard deviation of $u_i$ at 1.8138 ($\pi\sqrt{3}$). (That is, the probit form 2.6 is the distribution function for a normal random variable with mean zero and variance one, while the logit expression 2.5 is the distribution function of a logistic random variable with variance $\pi^2/3$.) The import of this in terms of interpretation is that the latent values $Y_i^*$ and marginal effects $b_k$ have only ordinal, not cardinal, meaning. (It also suggests something about a comparison of probit and logit coefficients, as will be noted below.)

If this latent preference structure is applicable in a particular example and the primary focus is on the behavior of latent preferences, we need go no further in our interpretation of the models to make effective use of probit and logit analysis. But if our interest centers on choice probabilities rather than latent preferences, we require further interpretation. The dichotomous and polytomous cases are considered separately below.

## 2.5.1 INTERPRETATION OF THE DICHOTOMOUS PROBIT AND LOGIT MODELS

In regression, $b_k$ measures the effect of exogenous variable k on the average value of Y. And the average value of a dichotomous variable is

TABLE 2.1

Illustrative Values of Probit and Logit for
Dichotomous Model with Two Exogenous Variables

| | | | Probit | | | Logit | | |
|---|---|---|---|---|---|---|---|---|
| X1 | X2 | X3 | Z | P (Y=1) | PHI | Z | P (Y=1) | P (1−P) |
| 1. | 1. | 0. | −2.00 | 0.02275 | 0.05399 | −3.60 | 0.02660 | 0.02589 |
| 1. | 3. | 0. | −1.00 | 0.15865 | 0.24197 | −1.80 | 0.14185 | 0.12173 |
| 1. | 5. | 0. | 0.0 | 0.50000 | 0.39894 | −0.00 | 0.50000 | 0.25000 |
| 1. | 7. | 0. | 1.00 | 0.84135 | 0.24197 | 1.80 | 0.85815 | 0.12173 |
| 1. | 9. | 0. | 2.00 | 0.97725 | 0.05399 | 3.60 | 0.97340 | 0.02589 |
| 1. | 1. | 1. | −1.00 | 0.15865 | 0.24197 | −1.80 | 0.14185 | 0.12173 |
| 1. | 3. | 1. | 0.0 | 0.50000 | 0.39894 | −0.00 | 0.50000 | 0.25000 |
| 1. | 5. | 1. | 1.00 | 0.84135 | 0.24197 | 1.80 | 0.85815 | 0.12173 |
| 1. | 7. | 1. | 2.00 | 0.97725 | 0.05399 | 3.60 | 0.97340 | 0.02589 |
| 1. | 9. | 1. | 3.00 | 0.99865 | 0.00443 | 5.40 | 0.99550 | 0.00448 |
| 1. | 1. | 2. | 0.0 | 0.50000 | 0.39894 | −0.00 | 0.50000 | 0.25000 |
| 1. | 3. | 2. | 1.00 | 0.84135 | 0.24197 | 1.80 | 0.85815 | 0.12173 |
| 1. | 5. | 2. | 2.00 | 0.97725 | 0.05399 | 3.60 | 0.97340 | 0.02589 |
| 1. | 7. | 2. | 3.00 | 0.99865 | 0.00443 | 5.40 | 0.99550 | 0.00448 |
| 1. | 9. | 2. | 4.00 | 0.99997 | 0.00013 | 7.20 | 0.99925 | 0.00075 |

Models Probit: $Z = -2.5X1 + .5X2 + 1.0X3$
Logit: $Z = -4.5X1 + .9X2 + 1.8X3$

equal to the probability that it assumes the value one. Thus in the linear probability model, $b_k$ measures the effect on $P(Y = 1)$ of a unit change in $X_k$, and this effect is the same for all values of $X_k$ (and all values of all other $X_k$'s) since the model is linear. (Note that the i subscript is deleted for the remainder of this chapter.) In logit and probit, the nonlinearity of the relationship between $P(Y = 1)$ and each $X_k$ means that the interpretation of the impact of a change in $X_k$ on $Pr(Y = 1)$ is less straightforward.

The behavior of the functional forms for the logit and probit probabilities is most easily seen with an example. Table 2.1 contains illustrative values for both functions in a model with two exogenous variables and a constant (K = 3).

The first three columns display the constant term ($X_1$) and the various values of the other two variables. The values of the three coefficients ($b_k$) vary between the logit and probit models and are indicated at the foot of the table. Columns four and seven contain values of Z ($Z = \Sigma b_k X_k$) computed using the probit and logit coefficients respectively. $P(Y = 1)$, computed according to equations 2.6 and 2.5, appears in columns five and eight. Note that $P(Y = 1)$ is exactly one half when Z is 0 in both models and both curves are symmetric about that point.

The Z values are linear functions of the exogenous variables and thus change with each $X_k$ according to the sign and magnitude of the corresponding $b_k$. As seen in the table, $P(Y = 1)$ varies directly with Z, ranging from near 0 at large negative values of Z to near 1 at large positive values. But note that the rate of change is not constant. When Z is large and negative, $P(Y = 1)$ increases only slowly with Z; at values of Z near zero the rate of change in $P(Y = 1)$ is high; and when Z is large and positive $P(Y = 1)$ again increases slowly. Connecting $X_k$ and $P(Y = 1)$, then, we see that $b_k$ determines the direction of effect, but the magnitude of the effect depends on the magnitude of Z, and that depends in turn on the magnitude of all of the $X_k$'s.

Since its effect is not constant, assessing the impact of $X_k$ on $P(Y = 1)$ requires some effort. One way to do this is to select interesting values of the exogenous variables and compute the associated $P(Y = 1)$, vary the $X_k$ of interest by some small amount and recompute the $P(Y = 1)$, and then measure the rate of change as $dP(Y = 1)/dX_k$, where $dP(Y = 1)$ indicates the difference in the two computed values of $P(Y = 1)$ and $dX_k$ is the corresponding difference in the chosen $X_k$. When $dX_k$ is very small, this rate of change is simply the derivative of $P(Y = 1)$ with respect to $X_k$, and formulas for it in the probit and logit cases respectively are given by[26]

$$\frac{dP(Y = 1)}{dX_k} = \frac{1}{\sqrt{2\pi}} \exp(-Z^2/2)b_k \equiv \Phi(Z)b_k$$

$$\frac{dP(Y = 1)}{dX_k} = \frac{\exp(Z)}{1 + \exp(Z)} \cdot \frac{1}{1 + \exp(Z)} b_k$$

$$= P(Y = 1)[1 - P(Y = 1)] b_k \qquad [2.19]$$

In both models the term $b_k$ appears as a multiplicative factor and in fact determines the sign of the effect, since the other factor in each equation is necessarily positive. But the effect of $X_k$ on $P(Y = 1)$ is attenuated in both cases by a nonlinear function of Z (and thus all K of the $X_k$'s). The columns labeled PHI and P(1 – P) in Table 2.1 give this attenuation factor for the probit and logit forms respectively. Notice that the attenuation is at a minimum when Z is zero and increases as Z grows large, positively or negatively.

Thus we see that the effect of a change in $X_k$ on the probability of the response Y = 1 is clearly related to, though not completely determined by, $b_k$. The sign of $b_k$ determines the direction of the effect, and the effect tends to be larger, the larger is $b_k$. So qualitatively the interpretation of $b_k$ is the same as in the linear regression model. But since the magnitude of the effect varies with the values of the exogenous variables, description of that effect is not so simple. Often it will entail the employment of tables or graphs showing the range of values of $dP/dX_k$ corresponding to various values of X. One might, for example, produce a table much like Table 2.1 which contains, for various interesting values of the exogenous variables, the computed for Z, the choice probability and the attenuation factor.

Finally, we can use Table 2.1 to compare logit and probit. The similarity of the two models is obvious, but note that the closeness of $P(Y = 1)$ in the two models results from a carefully chosen scaling of the coefficients used in the illustration. As noted above, the models employ normalization factors of 1 and 1.8138 in probit and logit respectively. Since the ratio of these two factors is approximately 1.8, the coefficient values chosen for the entries in Table 2.1 were such that the three logit coefficients were a multiple (1.8) of the corresponding probit coefficients (and thus the value Z for logit was 1.8 times the value of Z for probit). In a similar manner, probit and logit analysis applied to the same set of data should produce coefficient estimates which differ approximately by a factor of proportionality, and that factor should be about 1.8. (Amemiya [1981] suggests a scale difference of about 1.6. This constant is the ratio of the attenuation factors for probit and logit at $Z = 0$ and may be a better representation of the coefficient differences for data with few extreme values.)

### 2.5.2 INTERPRETATION OF THE POLYTOMOUS LOGIT MODEL

Table 2.2 contains illustrative values for a trichotomous (J = 3) logit model. With three alternatives and two exogenous variables plus a constant, there are 9 coefficients $b_{jk}$ in the model, three of which are fixed at 0 by the normalization rule. The selected values of the 6 nonzero coefficients are indicated at the base of the table. Selected values of the two exogenous variables are indicated in the first two columns of the table. With three alternatives, there are three preference indicators ($Z_1$, $Z_2$, and $Z_3$); the first two of these are shown in columns 3 and 4 while the third is always 0. As seen in the table, the preference indicators ($Z_1$ and $Z_2$) change with the exogenous variables according to the sign and magnitude of the corresponding coefficients, and the magnitude of the change is constant at all levels of the exogenous variables. For example, $Z_1$ increases by two units for every one unit change in $X_2$, and $Z_2$ decreases by one unit for every one unit increase in $X_3$.

## TABLE 2.2
### Illustrative Values for Trichotomous Logit Model with Two Exogenous Variables

| X2 | X3 | Z1 | Z2 | P(Y=1) | P(Y=2) | P(Y=3) | P1/P2 | P1/P3 | P2/P3 |
|----|----|------|------|--------|--------|--------|-------|-------|-------|
| 0. | 0. | -3.0 | 0.0 | .0243 | .4879 | .4879 | .0498 | .0498 | 1.000 |
| 1. | 0. | -1.0 | 1.0 | .0900 | .6652 | .2447 | .1353 | .3679 | 2.718 |
| 2. | 0. | 1.0 | 2.0 | .2447 | .6652 | .0900 | .3679 | 2.718 | 7.389 |
| 3. | 0. | 3.0 | 3.0 | .4879 | .4879 | .0243 | 1.000 | 20.09 | 20.09 |
| 4. | 0. | 5.0 | 4.0 | .7275 | .2676 | .0049 | 2.718 | 148.4 | 54.60 |
| 0. | 1. | -1.0 | -1.0 | .2119 | .2119 | .5761 | 1.000 | .3678 | .3678 |
| 1. | 1. | 1.0 | 0.0 | .5761 | .2119 | .2119 | 2.718 | 2.718 | 1.000 |
| 2. | 1. | 3.0 | 1.0 | .8438 | .1142 | .0420 | 7.389 | 20.09 | 2.718 |
| 3. | 1 | 5.0 | 2.0 | .9465 | .0471 | .0064 | 20.09 | 148.4 | 7.389 |
| 4. | 1 | 7.0 | 3.0 | .9811 | .0180 | .0009 | 54.60 | 1097. | 20.09 |
| 0. | 2. | 1.0 | -2.0 | .7054 | .0351 | .2595 | 20.09 | 2.718 | .1353 |
| 1. | 2. | 3.0 | -1.0 | .9362 | .0171 | .0466 | 54.60 | 20.09 | .3679 |
| 2. | 2. | 5.0 | 0.0 | .9867 | .0066 | .0066 | 148.4 | 148.4 | 1.000 |
| 3. | 2. | 7.0 | 1.0 | .9966 | .0025 | .0009 | 403.4 | 1097. | 2.718 |
| 4. | 2. | 9.0 | 2.0 | .9990 | .0009 | .0001 | 1097. | 8103. | 7.389 |

X1 is the constant term, Z1 = −3 + 2X2 + 2X3, and Z2 = 0 + X2 − X3

The probabilities associated with the three alternatives appear in columns five-seven. The first of these probabilities, $P(Y = 1)$, moves in the same direction as does $Z_1$ at all values of $X_2$ and $X_3$, though the magnitude of the change varies with both $Z_1$ and $Z_2$. Thus $P(Y = 1)$ is seen to respond to the exogenous variables very much like the probability of a positive response in a dichotomous logit model.

$P(Y = 2)$, on the other hand, is less well behaved. For example, when $X_3$ is 1, increases in $X_2$ cause $P(Y = 2)$ to fall even though the relevant co-efficient ($b_{22}$) is positive. And when $X_3$ equals 0, increases in $X_2$ at first cause $P(Y = 2)$ to rise but later cause it to fall. The reason for this apparent anomaly is that the three probabilities must always be positive and sum to one. Increases in $X_2$ tend to cause both $P(Y = 1)$ and $P(Y = 2)$ to rise, since $b_{12}$ and $b_{22}$ are both positive. And if these two probabilities rise, the third must fall. But when the third probability approaches 0, it can fall little more; further increases in either $P(Y = 1)$ or $P(Y = 2)$ must come at the expense of the other one. Since $b_{12}$ is greater than $b_{22}$ ($b_{12} = 2$ while $b_{22} = 1$), $Z_1$ rises more rapidly than $Z_2$ and accordingly $P(Y = 1)$ rises at the expense of $P(Y = 2)$. The behavior of $P(Y = 3)$ is likewise irregular and for similar reasons.

This result, that the signs of the coefficients $b_{jk}$ are not sufficient to determine the direction of change of the corresponding probabilities, necessitates increased care in interpretation of the results of polytomous logit models. In the discussion of the dichotomous model immediately above, we examined the derivatives of the probability expressions to detect the rate of change of the probabilities in response to changes in exogenous variables. Unfortunately, doing the same thing here yields expressions too complicated to be of much use in describing the results of polytomous logit analysis.

A more practical view of the behavior of the polytomous prob-abilities is one which focuses not on the probabilities themselves but rather on their ratios (that is on the odds of one event relative to another). From equation 2.15 we see that the odds for the event $Y = j$, relative to the event $Y = j'$, is given by

$$\frac{P(Y = j)}{P(Y = j')} = \frac{\exp(\Sigma b_{jk} X_k)}{\exp(\Sigma b_{j'k} X_k)} = \exp[\Sigma(b_{jk} - b_{j'k})X_k] \qquad [2.20]$$

We are interested in the behavior of these odds as the exogenous variables change. Since the function $\exp(\cdot)$ increases as its argument increases, the difference in the two coefficients alone determines the direction of change of the odds ratio as the exogenous variable changes.

The result above provides an easy and straightforward method for interpreting the results of logit analysis for polytomous models. Consider two alternatives, say j and j', and one exogenous variable, say $X_k$. If the difference in the two relevant coefficients, $b_{jk} - b_{j'k}$, is positive, then increases in the exogenous variable will increase the likelihood of observing alternative j rather than alternative j'. (Note that we speak here only of relative probabilities. Both probabilities may rise, so long as $P(Y = j)$ rises by more than $P(Y = j')$, or both may fall, so long as $P(Y = j)$ falls by less than $P(Y = j')$.)

While simple and straightforward, this means of comparison has two limitations. First, it tells only of relative changes; if information is required on the probabilities themselves, there is no alternative but to compute those probabilities at selected values of the variables. Second, it provides only for comparing alternatives one pair at a time.

The last three columns of Table 2.2 display all three possible odds ratios for the trichotomous case and serve to illustrate the use of this concept. As is seen there, all three odds ratios increase with both $X_2$ and $X_3$ with the exception of one case; for a fixed value of $X_2$, increases in $X_3$ cause the odds ratio $P(Y = 2)/P(Y = 3)$ to decline. This is because the coefficient values chosen for the illustration yield positive differences in five of the six cases. (For example, since $(b_{12} - b_{22} = 2 - 1)$ is positive, $P(Y = 1)/P(Y = 2)$ must rise with $X_2$.) Of the six pairs, only $(b_{23} - b_{33} = -1 - 0)$ is negative, so that $P(Y = 2)/P(Y = 3)$ falls as $X_3$ increases.

## 2.6 Summary

The purpose of this chapter was to develop nonlinear alternatives to the linear probability model. We presented seven alternatives and indicated how some might apply to some circumstances (e.g., the Burr if $Z_i$ is only positive, the Gompertz if asymmetries are involved, logit, probit, and Urban's curve if symmetry and both positive and negative values are reasonable, and so forth). We then showed how these alternative specifications can be rooted in a choice model of behavior (emphasizing that it is not necessary to assume the choice model). We also indicated why probit and logit are the most common models employed, and that logit (and, for practical purposes, only logit) can be extended to the polytomous case and that it also can be derived from a behavioral choice-type model. Having dealt with specification, it is now time to consider estimation of probit and logit.

## 3. ESTIMATION OF PROBIT AND LOGIT MODELS FOR DICHOTOMOUS DEPENDENT VARIABLES

### 3.0 Introduction

Now that the basic conception of the nonlinear models for estimation with a binary dependent variable has been covered, it is time to turn to the problem of estimation of these models. This chapter covers estimation of parameters for the probit and the logit model. As discussed in the last chapter, these two models are but two of many that have been proposed as nonlinear alternatives to the Linear Probability Model. These two are, however, the two most developed, and therefore most common and widely available alternatives. In this chapter, we will examine the methods of estimation, and the like, assuming that the data are a random sample of unreplicated data with a dichotomous Y. These methods serve as prototypes for corresponding procedures for replicated data samples and for variables with polytomous outcomes.

### 3.1 Assumptions of the Models

The dependent random variable, Y, is assumed to be binary, taking on but two values, say 0 and 1. The outcomes on Y are assumed to be mutually exclusive and exhaustive. The question of interest hinges on the value of the parameter P, the probability that Y equals one (or P = P(Y = 1)).

Y is assumed to depend on K observable variables $X_k$, k = 1, . . . , K. That is, the exogenous variables, we assume, account for the variation in P.[27] We can indicate this relationship by writing P = P(Y = 1 | $X_1$, . . . , $X_k$), or simply P = P(Y | X), where X denotes the set of K independent variables. This assumption is analogous to the standard regression model in which the exogenous variables account for the variation in the mean, or expectation, of Y.

The next assumption in OLS regression would be that Y and X are linearly related. Here, of course, we make quite different assumptions about the exact relationship between the endogenous variable (Y) and X. The probit model is given by:

$$P(Y = 1 | X) = \Phi(\Sigma b_k X_k) = \int_{-\infty}^{\Sigma b_k X_k} \exp(-u^2/2)/\sqrt{2\pi} \, du \qquad [3.1]$$

and the logit model is:

$$P(Y = 1 | X) = \exp(\Sigma b_k X_k)/[1 + \exp(\Sigma b_k X_k)] \qquad [3.2]$$

The remaining unknowns, then, are the parameters $b_k$, k = 1, ..., K. (Denote this set of K parameters by $b$.) The parallel with OLS is that, in both cases, a particular form of the relationship between Y and $X$ is assumed up to the unknown parameters $b$. The set of assumptions made so far can be called the "specification" assumptions.

As in OLS regression, we assume that the data are generated from a random sample of size N, with a sample point denoted by i, i = 1, ..., N. This assumption requires that the observations on Y be statistically independent of each other, ruling out serial correlation. (An assumption analogous to homoscedasticity or constant variance in OLS regression is not needed here since it is implicit in equations 3.1 and 3.2 above.)

As in OLS, the independent variables may be random variables, for example responses to survey questions, or they may be fixed, as in an experimental setting. We require only that there be no exact linear dependence among the $X_{ik}$'s. This assumption implies that N > K, that each $X_k$ must have some variation across observations (apart from the constant term), and that no two or more $X_k$'s be perfectly correlated. These assumptions are exactly the same as those made in OLS. And, like that model, if near though not exact linear dependencies exist, then problems of computational imprecision, unstable estimates, and large sampling error may occur. That is, probit and logit suffer the same problems of multicollinearity as does OLS regression.

The above assumptions may be summarized as follows (noting the parallels with OLS as in, for example, Lewis-Beck [1980, p. 26]):

(i)     $Y_i \epsilon \{0, 1\}$, i = 1, ..., N

(ii-a)  $P(Y_i = 1|X_i) = \Phi(\Sigma b_k X_{ik})$   (unit normal c.d.f.) for probit or

(ii-b)  $P(Y_i = 1|X_i) = \dfrac{\exp(\Sigma b_k X_{ik})}{1 + \exp(\Sigma b_k X_{ik})}$   for logit

(iii)   $Y_1, Y_2, ..., Y_N$ are statistically independent

(iv)    No exact or near linear dependencies exist among the $X_{ik}$s across K

## 3.2 Maximum Likelihood Estimation

Probit and logit parameters are typically estimated by a method called Maximum Likelihood Estimation (MLE) in contrast to ordinary regression models which are estimated by the method of Least Squares Estimation (LSE) (or OLS if the "ordinary," Gauss-Markov assumptions are made).[28]

All LSE methods try to find parameter estimates ($\hat{b}_k$'s in this case) that make the predicted values of Y, based on the parameter estimates and the assumed relationship between Y and $X$, as close as possible to the actually observed values of Y. In OLS, closeness is measured by the sum of squared differences between observed and predicted values of Y. In particular, as possible values of $\hat{b}$ are tried out, each set of values gives rise to an error in the fit for each observation. These errors are squared and then summed over all N observations. The OLS estimates $\hat{b}_k$, then, are those values of $b_k$ that make the sum of squared error the smallest possible (for that particular set of data).

The method of MLE has a different objective, but, given that objective, proceeds to derive estimates much like in OLS. The MLE objective can be explained as follows. Let $P_i = P(Y_i = 1 \mid X_i)$ as specified by equation 3.1 or 3.2 above. Then $P(Y_i = 0 \mid X_i) = 1 - P_i$, and the probability of observing outcome $Y_i$, whether it be 0 or 1, is given by $P(Y_i \mid X_i) = P_i^{Y_i}(1 = P_i)^{1-Y_i}$. Next note that the probability of observing a particular sample of N values of Y, say $Y$, given all N sets of values $X_i$, say $X$, is given by the product of the N probability expressions, since the observations are independent. That is,

$$P(Y \mid X) = \prod_{i=1}^{N} P_i^{Y_i}(1 - P_i)^{1-Y_i}.$$

Of course $P_i$, and thus $P(Y \mid X)$, depends on the values of the K coefficients in $b$. Since our objective is to estimate $b$, we proceed to make this dependence on $b$ explicit by defining the likelihood function, $L(Y \mid X, b) \equiv P(Y \mid X)$. If this function were to be evaluated, using the sample observations on $Y$ and $X$ and a particular numerical value (or set of K values) for $b$, it would yield a number between zero and one which would represent the probability, or likelihood, of observing that particular sample $Y$ if the employed value $b$ were indeed the "true" value. The principle of MLE, quite simply, is to choose as an estimate of $b$ that set of K numbers, say $\tilde{b}$, which would make the likelihood of having observed this particular $Y$ as large as possible. In particular, each "trial value" of $b$ will yield a value of $L(Y \mid X, b)$. We take as the MLE estimate $\tilde{b}$ that particular value (set of K numbers) for $b$ which yields the largest value, $L(Y \mid X, \tilde{b}) = \max_{b} L(Y \mid X, b)$.

Thus, the conceptual difference between OLS and MLE is that OLS is concerned with picking parameter estimates that yield the smallest sum of squared errors in the fit between the model and data, while MLE is concerned with picking parameter estimates that imply the highest probability or likelihood of having obtained the observed sample $Y$.

In OLS regression, the expression for the sum of squared errors is formed, the first derivative is computed and set to zero for each of the K coefficients, and the resulting K equations (the so called normal equations of OLS regression), are used to solve for the K unknowns, $b$. These solutions are the OLS estimates $\hat{b}$. In the standard linear model of Chapter 1, the OLS normal equations are:

$$\sum_{i=1}^{N} [Y_i - (\sum_k \hat{b}_k X_{ik})] \, X_{ij} = 0 \qquad j = 1, \ldots, K$$

WLS estimation proceeds in a similar manner, except that it starts with an expression for the *weighted* sum of squared errors. The WLS normal equations (recall that the linear probability model was solved by a WLS procedure) are:

$$\sum_{i=1}^{N} [Y_i - (\sum_k \hat{b}_k X_{ik})] \, W_i^2 \, X_{ij} = 0 \qquad j = 1, \ldots, K$$

In MLE we proceed to find $b$ so as to maximize the probit likelihood,

$$L(Y|X,b) = \prod_{i=1}^{N} [\Phi(\sum_k b_k X_{ik})]^{Y_i} [1 - \Phi(\sum_k b_k X_{ik})]^{1-Y_i}$$

or the logit likelihood,

$$L(Y|X,b) = \prod_{i=1}^{N} \left[ \frac{\exp(\sum_k b_k X_{ik})}{1 + \exp(\sum_k b_k X_{ik})} \right]^{Y_i} \left[ \frac{1}{1 + \exp(\sum_k b_k X_{ik})} \right]^{1-Y_i}$$

Since it is easier to work with sums than with products we start by taking logarithms,

$$\log L(Y|X,b) = \sum_{i=1}^{N} [Y_i \log P_i + (1 - Y_i) \log(1 - P_i)]$$

(Note that if $b$ maximizes $L(Y|X, b)$, it also maximizes $\log L(Y|X, b)$.) Then first derivatives are computed, with respect to each of the K coefficients $b_k$, and set equal to zero. Solution of these K equations, called the likelihood equations, will yield the MLE estimators. The equations for probit are:

$$\sum_{i=1}^{N} \frac{[Y_i - \Phi(\Sigma \hat{b}_k X_{ik})] \; \phi(\Sigma \hat{b}_k X_{ik})}{\Phi(\Sigma \hat{b}_k X_{ik}) \; [1 - \Phi(\Sigma \hat{b}_k X_{ik})]} \; X_{ij} = 0 \qquad j = 1, \ldots, K \qquad [3.5]$$

where $\phi(\cdot)$ is the probability density function for the standard normal distribution. (The density function is the derivative of the cumulative distribution function and in this case is $\Phi(a) = \exp(-a^2/\sigma)/\sqrt{2\pi}$). The likelihood equations for logit are:

$$\sum_{i=1}^{N} \left[ Y_i - \frac{\exp(\Sigma \hat{b}_k X_{ik})}{1 + \exp(\Sigma \hat{b}_k X_{ik})} \right] X_{ij} = 0 \qquad j = 1, \ldots, K \qquad [3.6]$$

Note that in both cases the likelihood equations are nonlinear in the $b_k$, so that explicit solutions cannot be obtained. The implications of this will be noted below.

The logit and probit likelihood equations can be written as:

$$\sum_{i=1}^{N} [Y_i - P(Y_i = 1|X_i, b)] \; A_i X_{ij} = 0 \qquad j = 1, \ldots, K$$

where $A_i = \phi/\Phi(1 - \Phi)$ for probit and $A_i = 1$ for logit.

The term inside the brackets is the deviation between the observation $Y_i$ and its expected or predicted value. As can be seen, then, all three estimators, MLE, WLS, and OLS, take as estimates those values of $\hat{b}$ which make a weighted sum of deviations between $Y_i$ and its expected value equal to zero. The differences are in the definition of the expected value of $Y_i$ ($\Sigma b_k X_{ik}$ in LSE and the LPM and $P(Y_i = 1|X_i, b)$ in logit and probit) and in the definition of the weights ($X_{ij}$, $W_i^2 X_{ij}$, and $A_i X_{ij}$ in the three cases).

## 3.3 Properties of Estimates

Derivation of the statistical properties of the MLE for logit and probit models is beyond the scope of this treatment. Rather, we merely state those properties, and in particular we contrast them with the statistical properties of the more familiar OLS and WLS estimators of the regression model.

The OLS estimator and its properties were reviewed in Chapter 1. To recap, if the assumptions of the standard linear model hold, then the OLS estimator is unbiased and efficient, within the class of linear, unbiased estimators. If, in addition, the disturbances are normally distributed, then the sampling distribution of the estimator is known and exact statistical tests are possible. If any of these assumptions fail, some or all of the properties are lost. The linear probability model serves to illustrate this latter claim and is of particular interest in and of itself. In the LPM, the homoscedasticity and normality assumptions are particularly untenable. The implication is that we should employ WLS, using estimated weights, rather than OLS. As was noted, use of estimated weights means that the statistical properties (unbiasedness, efficiency, normality) hold only as an approximation in large samples. Otherwise, little is changed from the methods of inference one would employ with OLS, *but only so long as* the central assumption ($E(Y_i) = P(Y_i = 1) = \Sigma b_k X_{ik}$) is maintained.

MLE is a visible alternative to OLS in nearly all situations to which the latter applies. For the general case, exact (small sample) properties of the MLE (unbiasedness, efficiency, normality) cannot be established. But it can be shown that, under conditions typically encountered, those properties hold approximately, with the quality of the approximation improving as the sample size grows. That is, the MLE exhibits the asymptotic (large sample) properties of unbiasedness, efficiency and normality. While for some special cases, exact results have been been obtained, probit and logit models are not among them. Still, for these models the large sample properties seem to hold reasonably well, even in moderate-sized samples on the order of $N - K = 100$.

WLS estimates of the LPM and MLE of logit or probit models thus both produce estimates with similar statistical properties, so statistical performance cannot be used as a basis of choice between the models. But in all cases, the statistical properties only hold given correctness of the corresponding assumptions. Since the only difference between the assumptions of the models lies in the specification of the mean value of Y (equations 1.7, 3.1, and 3.2), this becomes the key for choosing between the models and the estimation procedures.

A minor drawback to MLE on these models is that the likelihood equations for probit and logit are nonlinear in the parameters to be estimated (see equations 3.5 and 3.6). What that means, then, is that algebraic solutions are not obtainable. Rather, approximations by iterative algorithms are used.[29] These algorithms are readily available and use of them makes the extra computational effort transparent to the user.

To summarize the statements on statistical properties of MLE on probit and logit models, so long as its assumptions hold, these estimates have nearly the same properties as do OLS estimates of the regression model. The two differences are that the MLE on these models is nonlinear, thereby increasing computational costs, and that the properties are asymptotic, i.e., are better as sample size increases. The similarities, however, are striking. These similar properties are unbiasedness (the estimates are centered around the true values on average), efficiency (no other unbiased estimator has lower sampling variance), and normality (which means that we know how to perform hypothesis tests and draw other inferences). To make use of this later property, we need an estimate of the variances and covariances of the coefficient estimates. (In OLS, this matrix is estimated by $S^2(X'X)^{-1}$.) The appropriate estimate is the negative of the inverse of the matrix of second derivatives of the log-likelihood, which is typically computed as a part of the iterative maximization algorithm and is obtainable from most computer packages.

## 3.4 Interpretation of and Inference from MLE Results

To this point, we have specified the assumptions of the probit and logit models, derived estimates, and assessed their properties. Here, we discuss how to interpret and use the output from estimations.

### 3.4.1 STATISTICAL INFERENCE FROM PROGRAM OUTPUT

*(1) Individual Coefficient Estimates:* All routines, of course, report the parameter estimates $\hat{b}_k$ ($k = 1, \ldots, K$) and estimates of the associated standard errors $s_k$ ($k = 1, \ldots, K$). Some programs will provide, perhaps as an option, t-ratios $t_k$ ($k = 1, \ldots, K$) (alternatively referred to as standard normal variate ratios or z-scores), and perhaps a matrix or table of variances and covariances among all K coefficients, $s_{jk}$ ($j, k = 1, \ldots, K$).[30]

The point of probit and logit analysis is to measure the relationship between the exogenous variables, $X$, and the dependent variable, Y. Reported coefficient estimates are the asymptotically unbiased and efficient point estimates to be used for this purpose. Estimated standard errors provide the usual measure of the likely variation in the estimated coefficients that one might anticipate to arise from sample to sample. The analogy here between probit and logit and standard procedures such as linear regression is complete.

The t-statistic is used, just as in the usual regression case, for testing the null hypothesis that a coefficient, say $b_k$, is 0 (or equivalently that the variable $X_k$ has no effect on $Y^*$). This test statistic is defined as:

$$t_k = \hat{b}_k / s_k$$

(A more general form is $t_k = (\hat{b}_k - b_k^*) / s_k$ where $b_k^*$ is the hypothesized value of $b_k$ which need not be 0.) The interpretation of $t_k$ is straight-forward; values far from 0 contradict the null hypothesis and suggest rejection of it. The standard procedure is to compare this computed ratio to a one or two tailed critical value of the Student's t distribution with $N-K$ degrees of freedom and an arbitrary, a priori significance level (note that if the data are replicated, N would be replaced with the sum over $N_i$). If the computed statistic exceeds the critical value, the null hypothesis is rejected. Note that it is common to use the Student's t distribution, even though the coefficient estimates are only asymptotically normally distributed. The t is used to be more conservative in the hypothesis test than using the z-score test. A more conservative test in small samples seems warranted, given that the known distribution is only asymptotically normal. With large degrees of freedom the t distribution is equivalent to the normal, or more accurately, the t distribution is, like the distribution of coefficient estimates, asymptotically normal.

Confidence intervals about the parameter estimates can be constructed in the usual fashion. The appropriate formula is:

$$(C.I._k) = b_k \pm t_{(N-K;\alpha)} s_k \qquad [3.8]$$

*(2) Goodness of Fit:* In regression analysis, an F statistic (with $K-1$ and $N-K$ degrees of freedom) can be used to test the joint hypothesis that all coefficients except the intercept are zero. A corresponding test in logit and probit that suits exactly the same purpose is based on the likelihood ratio principle.[31] The method produces a statistic that follows, approximately, a chi-square distribution when the null hypothesis is true.[32] The likelihood ratio statistic is computed as:

$$c = -2\log(L0/L1) = (-2\log L0) - (-2\log L1) = -2(\log L0 - \log L1) \quad [3.9]$$

where L1 is the value of the likelihood function for the full model as fitted and L0 is the maximum value of the likelihood function if all coefficients except the intercept are 0. That is, the computed chi-square value tests the hypothesis that all coefficients except the intercept are 0, which is exactly the hypothesis that is tested in regression using the "overall" F statistic.

Canned programs vary to some extent in terms of the statistics actually reported for this joint hypothesis test. Many report the statistic $-2\log(L0/L1)$ directly (often denoted as $-2\mathrm{x}LLR$ or $-2$ times the log of the likelihood ratio). Sometimes only L1 is reported (either as L1 itself, or as $\log(L1)$, $-\log(L1)$ or $-2\log(L1)$). If L0 or some variant is not reported, it can be computed readily by the formula:

$$\log L0 = N0(\log(N0/N)) + N1(\log(N1/N)) \qquad [3.10]$$

where N is the sample size, N0 is the number of observations of $Y = 0$ and N1 is the number of cases in which $Y = 1$.[33] The degrees of freedom for this chi-square statistic is $K-1$ (i.e., the number of coefficients constrained to be zero in the null hypothesis). The formal test, then, is performed by comparing the computed statistic c to a critical value $(\chi^2(K-1, \alpha))$ taken from a table of the chi-square distribution with $K-1$ degrees of freedom and significance level $\alpha$.

In addition to a formal hypothesis test of goodness of fit, researchers using regression analysis are commonly interested in the $R^2$ value, or the value of the coefficient of determination. $R^2$ has a particularly attractive interpretation in regression as the proportion of the variance in the dependent variable that is "explained" by the exogenous variables. There is no statistic in probit or logit models with a comparable interpretation. In the regression model, the mean of the dependent variable and its variance are separate parameters. In regression, therefore, it is sensible to adjust the fitted mean (which depends on the coefficients) to match the mean of the dependent variable as observed in the sample data, choosing as coefficient estimates those values which minimize variance in fit. A reasonable measure of success in fit, then, is to measure the degree to which this error variance is minimized. The mean and variance are not separable parameters, however, in models with qualitative endogenous variables. A Bernoulli random variable, for example, has a mean of P and a variance of $P(1-P)$, so that the same parameter, P, appears in both. Thus, the variance is minimized at a P value of 0 or 1 regardless of the data (since the variance will be 0 by definition). Thus, minimizing variance is not a sensible criterion, and a measure of the proportion of variance explained is a useful one. Similarly, adjusting P so that the predicted mean fits the data better may lead to an increased error variance, again suggesting that minimizing error variance is not useful.

Nonetheless, there are a number of measures of goodness of fit in the spirit of $R^2$ that can be considered. For example, in the dichotomous case, predicted probabilities of a case being a 0 or a 1 are computed. We could make predictions based on the estimated $P_i$ terms. In particular, if $\hat{P}(Y = 1)$ is greater than .5, predict the case to be a 1, while if $\hat{P}(Y = 1)$ is less than .5 (and, therefore, the predicted $\hat{P}(Y = 0)$ will be greater than .5), predict that Y will be 0 in that case. These predictions can then be compared to the actual values of Y for each case, and one might be interested in the proportion of cases predicted correctly. There are, of course, well-known problems with that measure (Weisberg, 1978). In particular, there is no well-defined baseline or null expectation to measure the computed correct prediction rate against. In addition, an erroneous prediction when the estimated probability is, say, .51 may be considered a "smaller" error than an erroneous prediction based on estimated probability of .99. Nonetheless, this measure gives some clue as to the plausibility of the model. One might also examine a table of predicted versus actual values of the dependent variable (perhaps summarizing the table by some correlation coefficient). These sorts of measures are available on some canned probit and logit packages.

A number of pseudo-$R^2$ measures have been proposed and employed. One we propose here is defined as:

$$\text{pseudo } R^2 = c/(N + c) \qquad [3.11]$$

where c is the chi-square statistic for overall fit as described above, and N is the total sample size (where, if the data are replicated, the sum over $N_i$ should be substituted for N). This particular measure has two advantages. First, it is easily computed from readily available measures from virtually all programs. Second, it ranges between 0 and 1, approaching 0 as the quality of the fit diminishes (i.e., as c approaches 0) and 1 as it improves. This measure has two disadvantages as well. First, like the regression $R^2$, it does not incorporate a penalty for increasing the number of exogenous variables (one could make a correction for "degrees of freedom" similar to that used in regression, although this correction has no particular justification other than being a bit more conservative). Second, it is not universally accepted, let alone used.

McKelvey and Zavoina propose an $R^2$ measure, and their probit package reports it as an option (1975). As we did in Chapter 2, they make the analogy between probit and linear regression by examining the unobserved "variable," $Y^*$. Recall that $Y^*$, if observed, would be a linear function of the exogenous variables (i.e., $Y_i^* = \Sigma b_k X_{ik} + u_i$). It is this hypothetical variable $Y^*$ that is transformed by the cumulative normal in probit or the logistic transformation in logit. Given coefficient estimates, the term $\Sigma b_k X_{ik}$ can be computed, and its variance computed as well. This variance is analogous to the explained variance in regression. Next, recall that probit is arbitrarily normalized so that the variance of the stochastic term has a standard deviation of 1. Thus, it has a variance of 1. Summing all N cases, the "error variance," then, is equal to N. Finally, since it can be shown in regression that the explained and error variance are independent of each other, the total variance is equal to the sum of the explained and error variance. Thus, we have analogs for all terms in the standard formula for $R^2$:

$$R^2 = \text{Explained SS/ Total SS}$$

$$= \text{Explained SS/ (Explained SS + Error SS)}$$

where SS denotes sum of squares.

Let $\hat{Y}_i^* = \Sigma \hat{b}_k X_{ik}$, $\bar{Y} = \left( \sum_{i=i}^{N} Y_i^* \right) /N$, and $\text{ExSS} = \sum_{i-i}^{N} (\hat{Y}_i^* - \bar{Y})^2$

Then the McKelvey-Zavoina formula for pseudo $R^2$ for probit can be written as

$$\text{pseudo } R^2 = \text{ExSS}/(\text{ExSS} + N) \qquad [3.12a]$$

To modify the formula for the logit model, recall that the normalization employed in logit fixes the disturbance standard deviation at 1.814 (variance = 3.29). The error sum of squares is thus N times this variance, and the appropriate formula for logit, using the same definition of ExSS, is

$$\text{pseudo } R^2 = \text{ExSS}/(\text{ExSS} + 3.29N) \qquad [3.12b]$$

Either formulation of $R^2$ type measures have disadvantages, as do others that have been proposed. The most consequential criticism is probably that no one measure is universally accepted or employed (combined with the belief by many that no such measure should be employed). If a particular statistic is to be of use, especially one for comparing the fit of different models, it must be widely used and recognized. Thus, the usefulness of these or any summary measure, apart from formal test statistics, is diminished. Moreover, as in the regression $R^2$, even a good summary measure can be misinterpreted. Our recommendation, therefore, is to use summary measures with extreme caution, if at all.

*(3) Joint Hypothesis Tests for Subsets of Coefficients:* To this point, we have defined procedures for testing hypotheses about individual coefficients and about the set of all coefficients except the intercept. In many circumstances, hypotheses of interest center on the importance or significance of more than one coefficient, but not all of them. For example, variables $X_3$, $X_4$, and $X_5$ might be dummy variables indicating the religion of a survey respondent. The t test defined in point 1 above can be used to test the difference between pairs of religions in their effect on Y (or one could examine whether confidence intervals overlap, suggesting the impact of the coefficients in that pair are not significantly different). However, this procedure does not provide a proper test of the joint effect of the three variables, or, to continue the illustration, the total effect of religion on Y. Further, one might conclude that each of the three coefficients taken alone is not significantly related to Y, but that conclusion does not support the assertion that the three variables together do not have a significant impact on Y. There are two procedures that can be used to test joint hypotheses.

The first procedure is a variant on the likelihood ratio test reported above for the overall fit of the model. Take, as an example, the hypothesis that $b_3$, $b_4$, and $b_5$ are 0, while all other coefficients are allowed to assume their MLE value. The fitted likelihood is the same L1 as before (i.e., the likelihood given the data and given that all coefficients are allowed to go to their MLE value). This likelihood is to be compared to the likelihood value that results from constraining the coefficients $b_3$, $b_4$, and $b_5$ to be zero, leaving the other coefficients unconstrained. Call this constrained likelihood L2. (L2 can be obtained by reestimating the model excluding the three religion variables. L2 will be the fitted likelihood for this smaller model. Note that estimated values of other coefficients will change.) Then the quantity

$$c = -2\log(L2/L1) \qquad [3.13]$$

will follow a chi-square distribution with three degrees of freedom (or more generally with degrees of freedom equal to the number of constraints imposed) if the null hypothesis is true. In particular, L2 can be no larger than L1, and will be equal to L1 only if the three coefficients of interest have coefficients of zero in the unconstrained model. The smaller L2 (and hence the larger the c statistic) the less likely it is that the three constrained coefficients are in fact zero. Similar statistics can be computed for other hypotheses which can be expressed as a set of constraints on coefficients of the model.

A difficulty with the test noted above is that it typically requires two estimation passes to construct the statistic, one to get the unconstrained likelihood and a second to get the likelihood with constraints. An alternative test can be computed from the output of one pass, provided the computer routine makes the variance-covariance matrix for the parameter estimates available. Suppose the null hypothesis is that some J of the coefficients $b_k$ are zero (where J is taken to be less than $K-1$). Let $S_J$ represent the J by J matrix containing the estimated variances and covariances of those coefficients, and let $\hat{b}_J$ represent the set (vector) of the J coefficient estimates. (Clearly, the order of the elements in $\hat{b}_J$ should correspond to the arrangement of rows and columns in $S_J$.) Then, the computed value:

$$c = \hat{b}_J' \, S_J^{-1} \, \hat{b}_J$$

is a statistic that follows a chi-square distribution with J degrees of freedom if the null hypothesis is correct.[34] (As before, the more general formulation would have $b_J - b_J{}^*$ in place of $b_J$ in the above formula, where where $b_J{}^*$ denotes the set of hypothesized values for the J coefficients.) For example, let the null hypothesis be that $b_4 = b_7 = 0$. The statistic is computed according to

$$c = (\hat{b}_4, \hat{b}_7) \begin{bmatrix} s_{44} & s_{47} \\ s_{74} & s_{77} \end{bmatrix}^{-1} \begin{bmatrix} \hat{b}_4 \\ \hat{b}_7 \end{bmatrix} = \frac{\hat{b}_4^2 \, s_{77} + \hat{b}_7^2 \, s_{44} - 2\hat{b}_4 \hat{b}_7 \, s_{47}}{s_{44} s_{77} - s_{47} s_{74}}$$

Since the hypothesis imposes two constraints, we would compare the computed value of c to a critical value taken from a table of the chi square with $J = 2$ degrees of freedom. The test is, of course, general, and can be used with any arbitrary number of coefficients.

The two tests we have proposed can be shown to be equivalent in the statistical sense, though they yield different numerical results. Note that if the latter test is constructed for a single coefficient, the result is the square of the t ratio described at the beginning of this section, and the two tests are identical.[35] Note also the parallel with standard tests of joint hypotheses in linear regression. The types of formulas employed here have their direct counterparts in ordinary regression problems.

### 3.4.2 AN EXAMPLE

Above we employed data gathered by Spector for examining the effect of a PSI teaching method in a Linear Probability Model analysis. The same data are examined here with probit and logit. Table 3.1 contains the results from a canned probit program, while Table 3.2 reports the results from a logit routine. In both cases, the tables are nearly verbatim reproductions of the actual printout to illustrate the kinds of information the user is likely to actually encounter. Table 3.3 gives direct comparisons among the three sets of estimates.

Let us examine first the goodness of fit of the models as estimated by probit, logit, and the LPM (see section 1.2.2). For the two estimation techniques of probit and logit, the chi-square statistic is essentially the same, 15.54 and 15.4 respectively, with 3 degrees of freedom. The probability of the null hypothesis being true, therefore, for either model, is less than .005. (Note that dividing these $\chi^2$s by 3 to produce "asymptotic F" statistics with 3 and 28 degrees of freedom yields essentially the same answer, though at a reduced significance level of about .02.) This result compares favorably with the F test for the LPM estimation, which was also significant beyond the .005 level. The WLS estimates yielded an $R^2$ value of about .376. Using the formula for our suggested pseudo-$R^2$ described above in equation 3.11, we find that probit and logit estimates yielded an $R^2$ of about .325, again quite comparable to the WLS estimates of the LPM model. We have also reported the percent of cases correctly predicted by all three procedures. Logit and probit made the same predictions for each case, while the LPM model predicted one more Y = 1 outcome correctly.[36] (Parenthetically, the predicted probability of Y being a 1 in that case for logit and probit was a bit more than .48, while it was about .53 in the LPM estimates, thus raising the question of how "severe" a mistake that was for probit and logit.) Obviously, the three models fit the data at almost the same levels. There is a very slight suggestion that the LPM fit is better than either logit or probit. However, the LPM model, even after truncation in the first round of the estimation, yielded four estimated "probabilities" that were less than zero (or 12.5% of the 32 cases).

The first question (and the only really easy comparison between either probit or logit and LPM) to ask about the individual coefficient estimates is the test of the null hypothesis. This test is a one-tailed t test (one-tailed since the direction of the effect is anticipated for all three exogenous variables). For the GPA variable, the null would be rejected

**TABLE 3.1**
**MLE Results for Probit Model on PSI Data**

| Number of Observations | 32 | (Y=0: 21 | Y=1: 11) |
|---|---|---|---|

| Independent Variable | Sum | Mean |
|---|---|---|
| Intercept | 32.0 | 1.0 |
| GPA | 99.75 | 3.12 |
| TUCE | 702. | 21.94 |
| PSI | 14. | .44 |

| Iteration Number | 1 | Log of likelihood function | $-0.10D\ 48$ |
|---|---|---|---|

| Coefficient | Maximum Likelihood Estimate |
|---|---|
| 1 | $-5.8837$ |
| 2 | 1.3103 |
| 3 | 0.0357 |
| 4 | 1.1266 |

| Iteration Number | 5 | Log of likelihood function | $-12.8188$ |
|---|---|---|---|

| Coefficient | Maximum Likelihood Estimate |
|---|---|
| 1 | $-7.4523$ |
| 2 | 1.6258 |
| 3 | 0.05173 |
| 4 | 1.4263 |

The Iteration has converged

| Final Iteration | Log of likelihood function | $-12.8188$ | |
|---|---|---|---|
| Coefficient | Maximum Likelihood Estimate | Standard Error | |
| 1 | $-7.4523$ | 2.5423 | |
| 2 | 1.6258 | .6939 | |
| 3 | 0.0517 | .0839 | |
| 4 | 1.4263 | .5950 | |

| $(-2.0)$ times log likelihood ratio | 15.545 | Degrees of freedom 3 |
|---|---|---|

for probit and logit if the $\alpha$ level were set between .01 and .025. In the LPM model, GPA is significant at the more stringent level of .0001. The variable of most interest, PSI (the new teaching method dummy variable), has an estimated effect in probit and logit at the same $\alpha$ level as the GPA variable, i.e., between .025 and .01. In the LPM, PSI appeared significant at the .001 level. The TUCE variable (the score on a test given at the beginning of the term) was found to affect significantly the final grade at the .0123 level in the LPM estimated model. This variable is not

**TABLE 3.2**
**MLE Results for Logit Model on PSI Data**

| Logit Analysis, | 32 Observations, 3 Independent Variables, 2 Groups | | |
|---|---|---|---|

| | Alternative | | |
| *Variable Means* | *1* | *2* | *Overall* |
|---|---|---|---|
| Number of Observations | 21 | 11 | 32 |
| 1 GPA | 2.952 | 3.433 | 3.117 |
| 2 TUCE | 21.09 | 23.545 | 21.935 |
| 3 PSI | 0.286 | 0.727 | 0.437 |

Fitting Constants Only

| Initial Logit Coefficients | | −2 Log Likelihood | 41.18 |
|---|---|---|---|
| 0 Constant | 0.64 | | |
| 1 GPA | 0.0 | | |
| 2 TUCE | 0.0 | | |
| 3 PSI | 0.0 | | |

Using Newton Method without Davidon's Update

| Iteration 1 | −2 Log Likelihood | 27.26 |
|---|---|---|
| 0 Constant | 8.1364 | |
| 1 GPA | −1.8704 | |
| 2 TUCE | −0.0426 | |
| 3 PSI | −1.6720 | |

. . .

| Iteration 5 | −2 Log Likelihood | 25.78 |
|---|---|---|
| 0 Constant | 13.014 | |
| 1 GPA | −2.8245 | |
| 2 TUCE | −0.0951 | |
| 3 PSI | −2.3780 | |

Final Iteration

| | Coefficients | *Asymptotic Standard Errors* | *Asymptotic T-Ratios* |
|---|---|---|---|
| 0 Constant | 13.02 | 4.929 | 2.642 |
| 1 GPA | −2.826 | 1.263 | −2.239 |
| 2 TUCE | −0.095 | 0.141 | −0.672 |
| 3 PSI | −2.379 | 1.064 | −2.235 |

−2 Log Likelihood    25.78

Overall Chi-Square, 3 degrees of freedom    15.40

Variance-Covariance Matrix

| | Constant | GPA | TUCE | PSI |
|---|---|---|---|---|
| Constant | 24.29 | | | |
| GPA | −4.569 | 1.594 | | |
| TUCE | −0.346 | −0.0369 | 0.02003 | |
| PSI | −2.356 | 0.4271 | 0.01488 | 1.133 |

**TABLE 3.3**
**Comparison of Probit, Logit, and LPM Estimates of PSI Data**

| Estimate of | LPM | Probit | Logit |
|---|---|---|---|
| GPA | .3982 | 1.626 | 2.826 |
| (s.e.) | (.0878) | (.6939) | (1.263) |
| t ratio | 4.523 | 2.343 | 2.238 |
| significant a level | .0001 | .025 | .025 |
| PSI | .3878 | 1.426 | 2.379 |
| (s.e.) | (.105) | (.595) | (1.06) |
| t ratio | 3.687 | 2.397 | 2.235 |
| a level | .001 | .025 | .025 |
| TUCE | .0122 | .0517 | .0952 |
| (s.e.) | (.0045) | (.0839) | (.1415) |
| t ratio | 2.676 | 0.616 | 0.672 |
| a level | .012 | NS | NS |
| Intercept | −1.309 | −7.452 | −13.021 |
| F or −2xLLR | 29.92 | 15.545 | 15.40 |
| degrees of freedom | 3,28 | 3 | 3 |
| significance beyond | .995 | .995 | .995 |
| $R^2$ / psuedo $R^2$ | .3755 | .3270 | .3249 |
| Percent correctly predicted | 84.4% | 81.2% | 81.2% |
| Yule's Q predicted/actual | .929 | .882 | .882 |

TABLES OF PREDICTED AND ACTUAL Y SCORES

LPM-via WLS
Predicted Y

| A C T U A L | | 0 | 1 | |
|---|---|---|---|---|
| | 0 | 18 | 3 | 21 |
| | 1 | 2 | 9 | 11 |
| | | 20 | 12 | 32 |

Probit & Logit
Predicted Y

| | | 0 | 1 | |
|---|---|---|---|---|
| | 0 | 18 | 3 | 21 |
| | 1 | 3 | 8 | 11 |
| | | 21 | 11 | 32 |

significant at conventional levels in either the probit or logit estimates. (Interestingly, that was the conclusion drawn from examining the OLS estimates of the LPM.)

Probit and logit coefficient estimates can not be compared to each other directly. As already noted, there is a scale difference between the two, such that logit coefficients are about 1.8 times the size of otherwise comparable probit results. Making this (approximate) correction indicates that the two sets of coefficients differ very little. For example, multiplying the probit coefficients by 1.8 yields a GPA coefficient estimate of 2.927 to compare to the logit 2.826. The TUCE comparison is .0931 for probit, .0952 for logit, while the PSI comparison is 2.567 for probit compared to 2.379 for logit. In short, both on goodness of fit grounds and on the grounds of individual parameter estimate comparisons, there is very little difference between the two procedures. As noted earlier, this similarity between logit and probit is commonplace. Only if there are a lot of observations at extreme probability values will the two estimation techniques differ noticeably, for the probit and logit functional bases are essentially identical at all but the tails of their respective distributions (and even there the differences are but slight).

Comparison of the size of coefficients between probit or logit and LPM is more difficult. Casual inspection indicates that the three coefficients for the three explanatory variables are of approximately the same size. For example, the coefficient for GPA is the largest in each of the three estimations, while that for PSI is nearly as large in the three cases (it is about 97% the size of the GPA coefficient in the LPM, 88% in probit, and 84% in logit). Finally, the TUCE coefficient is much smaller in all three cases (about 3.05% the size of the GPA coefficient in the LPM, 3.18% in probit, and 3.37% in logit).

Of more interest is the predicted probabilities for the dependent variable, based on the coefficient estimates. As we noted in Chapter 1, a student having a GPA of 3, scoring a 20 on the pre-class examination, and not taking the special course has a probability of receiving an A of about .127. The "treatment" effect of being a member of the special class increases the probability of receiving an A to .516. With the LPM, of course, there is a constant impact of PSI on the dependent variable. In particular, the PSI method increases the probability of receiving an A by .388. No such easy statement is possible for probit and logit, since the impact of any variable is nonlinear. However, for the same student (i.e., one who had a 3.0 GPA and a score of 20 on TUCE) who had a value of 0 for PSI, the probability that he or she would receive an A was only .067 (in both the probit and logit cases). If that student attended the special class, PSI = 1, the probability of receiving an A would increase to about .455, given the probit estimates, and to about .435, given the logit estimates.

*How are these p's obtained?*
*Why such fits between them?*

## 3.5 Conclusions

In this chapter, we discussed a large number of topics. First, we covered the method of estimation most commonly encountered in estimating qualitative models, the method of maximum likelihood. We then used that procedure to derive estimates of the unknown parameters for both the probit and the logit models. These can be shown to be identical to weighted *nonlinear* least squares estimates.

We then discussed the properties of estimators of the dichotomous probit and logit models. As with the use of maximum likelihood estimation in general, the properties are all asymptotic, i.e., valid only as approximations which improve as the sample size grows. It was noted that probit and logit estimations yield asymptotically unbiased and efficient estimates which are asymptotically distributed as normal variates.

Methods of hypothesis testing for single parameters, joint hypotheses and hypotheses about the goodness of fit of the model as a whole were presented. These were shown to parallel the procedures applicable to ordinary, linear regression. The same conclusion was drawn about the construction of confidence intervals. We noted that there was no close parallel, however, with OLS regression in terms of $R^2$ measures. We proposed some surrogate measures, but cautioned that the nature of the estimation problem renders all such measures problematic.

In the next chapter we will extend the model more briefly to the case of more than a dichotomous dependent variable. As we will see, the polytomous case follows similar lines as the dichotomous case considered in detail here. We also will examine replicated data, for which there is a different (and easier) estimation procedure, in addition to that developed in this chapter.

## 4. MINIMUM CHI-SQUARE ESTIMATION AND POLYTOMOUS MODELS

### 4.0 Introduction

The two objectives to this chapter are to introduce an alternative to maximum likelihood estimation called "minimum chi-square estimation" (or "Berkson-Theil weighted least squares")[37] and to extend the analysis to cover polytomous dependent variables. The first topic is introduced because the minimum chi-square procedure is computationally easier than the standard MLE, when it can be applied. We turn first to that procedure.

## 4.1 Minimum Chi-Square Estimation
## for Replicated, Dichotomous Data

"Replicated data" refers to a situation in which there are a number of observations on Y for *each* observation on the set of exogenous variables, $X_k$. For example, in a true experimental setting, there may be a small number of exogenous variables (the experimental setting controlling for others), and these may be controlled so that only a small number of distinct values are permitted. Than at each value of the control variables, the experiment is repeated, yielding multiple measurements on Y. In the Ostrom-Aldrich example discussed in Chapter 1, there is a single exogenous variable which takes on but five values, and there a number of observations on Y for each value of X. Finally, the situation may arise also, if somewhat artificially, when data have been grouped.[38]

As before, there are K exogenous variables (including the constant). There are a total of M, possibly unique, combinations of values that any observation can have on the exogenous variables. Since it is convenient to think of these values as defining cells in a contingency table, we will refer to the M observations as "cells." For example, the Ostrom-Aldrich data contains 5 cells, while a study of decisions to attend college which includes sex (male and female) and family income (measured as high, medium, and low), would include 6 cells if observations are made on students of both sexes at each income level. For notational ease, an observation on the K exogenous variables will be represented as $X_i$, where i ranges from 1 to M. Thus, $X_i$ represents the set or vector of K values, $X_{i1}, \ldots, X_{ik}$ in cell i. For each of the M cells, there are $N_i$ responses to, or replications on, Y (which is assumed dichotomous). $N_i$ may, of course, differ across cells. $N0_i$ represents the number of cases in cell i that take on a Y value of 0, while $N1_i$ indicates how many have a Y value of 1. Obviously, $N_i = N0_i + N1_i$. Further, the total number of replications, N, is

$$N = \sum_{i=1}^{M} N_i$$

Since the logit model is simpler to describe than the probit model, we turn to it first.

## 4.11 THE LOGIT MODEL

Let $P_i$ denote the probability that $Y = 1$ for each replication in cell i, given $X_i$. In Chapter 2, we introduced the logit transformation

$$\log[P_i/(1 - P_i)] = \Sigma b_k X_{ik} \equiv b'X_i \qquad [4.1]$$

Equation 4.1 defines the "true logit." (The notation $b'X_i$ is used here to represent $\Sigma b_k X_{ik}$.) The "logit" refers to the inverse of the logistic probability transformation, while the "true" is used to indicate that the set of k values $b$ are the true parameter values.

The true logits cannot be observed directly, of course. With replicated data, they can be estimated within each cell by using the sample proportion of 1's in that cell, i.e., by

$$p_i \equiv N1_i/N_i \qquad [4.2]$$

Using the sample proportions $p_i$ as estimates of $P_i$, we can define the "observed logits" as

$$L_i \equiv \log[p_i/(1 - p_i)] \qquad [4.3]$$

Now, the observed logits can be used as estimates of the true logits:

$$L_i = \log[P_i/(1 - P_i)] + u_i \qquad [4.4]$$

or,

$$L_i = b'X_i + u_i \qquad [4.5]$$

where $u_i$ represents, of course, the error in observation, while the last equation substitutes equation 4.1 into 4.4.[39]

Equation 4.5 expresses $L_i$ as a linear function, just as in a linear regression equation. The obvious question, then, is whether equation 4.5 can be estimated via ordinary regression procedures. The answer is that OLS estimates will be inefficient, but a convenient weighted least squares procedure will yield unbiased and efficient estimates (at least efficient in the class of linear, unbiased estimators). The analogy to, say, the LPM estimator described in Chapter 1 is quite close. First, there is no reason to assume that $X_i$ and $u_i$ are not independent (or, at least, no reason emerging from the logic leading to equation 4.5), just as there is no reason to assume that the observations on $X_i$ are exactly linearly dependent. If the logistic form is correct, then the stochastic term, $u_i$, will have a zero mean and will follow, approximately, a normal distribution when $N_i$ is large.

Thus, to this point, all assumptions for OLS hold. However, the variance of $u_i$ is not constant but is

$$V(u_i) = 1/[N_iP_i(1 - P_i)] \qquad [4.6]$$

As in the LPM, $V(u_i)$ varies as a function of $N_i$, $P_i$, and hence $X_i$. Thus, it has a heteroscedastic error term.[40] If equation 4.5 is estimated via OLS, the coefficient estimates will be unbiased but inefficient. The solution, of course, is to use a weighted least squares estimator. As with the LPM with replicated data, the sample proportion, $p_i$, can be used as an estimate of $P_i$, and these can be substituted into the expression for $V(u_i)$, as given above.

It is worth emphasizing, at this point, the similarities and differences between the LPM of Chapter 1 and the minimum chi-square estimator considered here. Both specify a linear relationship and both require WLS estimation because of heteroscedasticity. But the models employ different definitions of the dependent variable: the LPM uses $Y_i$, in unreplicated data, or $p_i$, in replicated data, as the dependent variable while minimum chi-square estimation of the logit model applies only to replicated data and uses a nonlinear transformation of $p_i[\log p_i/(1 - p_i)]$ as the dependent variable. And the nature of the heteroscedasticity is not the same: $V(u_i) = P_i(1 - P_i)/N_i$ in the LPM while $V(u_i) = 1/[N_iP_i(1 - P_i)]$ in the model here. So the weights to be used in WLS will not be the same.

To summarize, minimum chi-square estimation of the logit model with replicated data proceeds as follows:

a. Define the dependent variable as a log odds ratio, $L_i$, of the proportion $N1_i/N_i$ for each cell, i, as in equation 4.3.

b. Weight each observation by $[N_ip_i(1 - p_i)]$. That is, each observation on Y and each independent variable should be multiplied by the value $\sqrt{(N_iP_i)(1 - P_i)}$.[41]

c. Estimate these weighted data by OLS, regressing the weighted dependent variable on the K weighted exogenous variables. Note that the number of "observations" is M, the number of distinct values of $X_i$.

The results are interpreted as are any regression results with three exceptions. As with any weighted least squares procedure, the $R^2$ as a measure of goodness of fit is questionable. Second the interpretation of the parameter estimates should follow the same lines as for the dichotomous logit model, as discussed in section 2.5. Though equation 4.5

looks like a linear model, the probabilities $P_i$ are still nonlinear transformations of $X_i$. Finally, properties of these estimates hold only if the number of replications, $N_i$, is large for each i, i = 1, ..., M.[42] The number of cells, M, on the other hand, need not be large, though it clearly must exceed K.

### 4.1.2 THE PROBIT MODEL

In the probit specification, the selection probabilities are given by

$$P(Y = 1 \mid X_i) = \Phi(b'X_i) \qquad [4.7]$$

where $\Phi(\cdot)$ is the standard normal cumulative distribution function. The only two required modifications to the minimum chi-square estimator of the logit model are analogous expressions for the inverse probability transform of equation 4.1 and the variance of the error term representing the difference between the "observed" and "true probits" corresponding to equation 4.6. In the logit model, the inverse probability transformation was simply the natural logarithm of the odds ratio. But just as the normal CDF in equation 4.7 does not have a closed form representation (it involves an integral expression), neither does the inverse probit transformation. We write it as:

$$\Phi^{-1}(P_i) = b'X_i \qquad [4.8]$$

Again using the sample proportions

$$p_i = N1_i / N_i \qquad [4.9]$$

as estimates of $P_i$, we define the observed probit as

$$Q_i = \Phi^{-1}(p_i) \qquad [4.10]$$

Computer routines for the computation of $Q_i$ are readily available. Using equations 4.8 and 4.10 we can now write the regression equation as

$$Q_i = b'X_i + u_i \qquad [4.11]$$

where $u_i$ is the observation error. The variance of $u_i$ in this probit model is given by

$$V(u_i) = [(P_i)(1 - P_i)] / [N_i \phi_i^2] \qquad [4.12]$$

where $\phi_i$ is the normal density function evaluated as $\Phi^{-1}[P_i]$.

Aside from a different definition of the dependent variable (equation 4.10 in place of equation 4.4) and a different formula for the variances, the reciprocals of which are to be used as weights (equation 4.12 in place of equation 4.6), the analysis proceeds exactly as in the logit formulation.

### 4.1.3 AN EXAMPLE

The data presented in Table 1 of Chapter 1 are used to illustrate the Minimum Chi-Square estimation method for the logit model. To create replicated data, we collapsed GPA scores into three groups (less than 2.8, between 2.8 and 3.3, and greater than 3.3) and ignored the variable TUCE. The data on PSI is recorded as 0 and 1, and the GPA values assigned were the median GPA in the respective group. Such grouping is not a practice to be recommended, of course, but serves well for illustration.

The resulting contingency table is presented in Table 4.1. The first two columns contain the values of GPA and PSI for the six groupings on these two variables. Columns 3 and 4 contain the number of students (or replications, $N_i$) and the number of students who earned a grade of A (or $N1_i$). Remaining columns in the table are transformations of the first four. The proportion of $Y_i = 1$, $p_i$, appears in column 5 and the observed logit ($L_i$), computed according to equation 4.3, is in column 6. Note that the entry for $p_i$ in row 1 should be zero. Since such a value would make the logit undefined, we replaced it by .01.

The first set of regression results in the table are from the ordinary least squares regression of $L_i$ in column 6 on the two independent variables, GPA in column 1 and PSI in column 2. As noted above, this model, corresponding to equation 4.5, is heteroscedastic, so the OLS estimates are unbiased but not efficient, and the standard errors and t-ratios are not correct.

To apply the more appropriate weighted least squares requires a definition of the weight and a transformation of the dependent and independent variables. The numbers in column 7 are computed as

$$W = [N_i p_i (1 - p_i)]^{1/2}$$

This formula defines the reciprocal of the standard error of the observed logit, which is the correct weight for WLS. Columns 8, 9, and 10 are simply this weight times the GPA, PSI and LOGIT entries in columns 1, 2, and 6. (Note that the weight for row one is relatively small, so the arbitrary redefinition of $p_i$ noted above is seen to have little effect on the results.)

## TABLE 4.1
## Min-Chi-Square Estimation of Dichotomous Logit Model on PSI Data

A: Grouped Data on the Effectiveness of PSI on Grades

| GPA 1 | PSI 2 | N 3 | N1 4 | p=N1/N 5 | Logit 6 | Weight 7 | W-GPA 8 | W-PSI 9 | W-Logit 10 |
|---|---|---|---|---|---|---|---|---|---|
| 2.66 | 0. | 5 | 0 | 0.01 | −4.595 | 0.222 | 0.591 | 0.000 | −1.022 |
| 2.66 | 1. | 3 | 1 | 0.33 | −0.693 | 0.816 | 2.171 | 0.816 | −0.565 |
| 3.03 | 0. | 9 | 1 | 0.11 | −2.079 | 0.942 | 2.856 | 0.000 | −1.960 |
| 3.03 | 1. | 6 | 3 | 0.50 | 0.000 | 1.224 | 3.710 | 1.224 | 0.000 |
| 3.62 | 0. | 4 | 2 | 0.50 | 0.000 | 1.000 | 3.620 | 0.000 | 0.000 |
| 3.62 | 1. | 5 | 4 | 0.80 | 1.386 | 0.894 | 3.237 | 0.894 | 1.239 |

B: Least Squares Regression of Logit on GPA and PSI

| | Coefficient | Standard Error | T-Ratio |
|---|---|---|---|
| Intercept | −12.859 | 2.537 | −5.07 |
| GPA | 3.4266 | 0.8046 | 4.26 |
| PSI | 2.4559 | 0.6362 | 3.86 |

Analysis of Variance Due to

| | DF | SS | MS=SS/DF | F Ratio |
|---|---|---|---|---|
| Regression | 2 | 20.0575 | 10.0287 | 16.52 |
| Residual | 3 | 1.8211 | 0.6070 | |
| Total | 5 | 21.8786 | | |

C: Weighted Least Squares Regression of Logit on GPA and PSI

| | Coefficient | Standard Error | T-Ratio |
|---|---|---|---|
| Weight | −10.156 | 1.586 | −6.41 |
| W-GPA | 2.7325 | 0.4710 | 5.80 |
| W-PSI | 1.8873 | 0.3356 | 5.62 |

Analysis of Variance Due to

| | DF | SS | MS=SS/DF | F Ratio |
|---|---|---|---|---|
| Regression | 3 | 6.3879 | 2.1293 | 17.80 |
| Residual | 3 | 0.3587 | 0.1196 | |
| Total | 6 | 6.7466 | | |

WLS amounts to an OLS regression using this weighted data. That is, the weighted logit is regressed on the weight, the weighted gpa and the weighted psi without an intercept. (The coefficient of WEIGHT is interpreted as the intercept.) Results of this regression are reported at the bottom of Table 4.1. They should be contrasted with the maximum likelihood results on the unreplicated data as reported in Table 3.2. Some comparability is lost because the MLE results included one additional exogenous variable (though that variable had a very small and insignificant coefficient) and the grouping of observations on GPA required to present the data as replicated means that some information is sacrificed. Still, the results agree quite well. It is also worth noting the differences between the OLS and WLS results in Table 4.1. The coefficient estimates differ only a little, and there is no theoretical reason they should. But the standard errors differ by a factor of two, highlighting the concern over heteroscedasticity in the model and the inappropriateness of the OLS variance results.

## 4.2 Polytomous Dependent Variables

In this section, we examine the multinomial logit model. As we noted above, extending the probit model to handle polytomous dependent variables is essentially impractical due to severe computational computational complications. The focus here will be on replicated data. Unreplicated data can be thought of as the special case of replicated data when there is a single replication per cell.

We will continue to let $X_i$ represent the values taken on by the K independent variables, and assume that there are M distinct combinations of values observed, with i, i = 1, ..., M, being the observation subscript. In the dichotomous case, there were two values that Y could take on. In the polytomous case, there are J such values. How many such values can be handled is a practical problem determined by the program to be used and its data limitations. In the dichotomous case, there were K parameters to estimate. In the polytomous case, there are $K(J-1)$ parameters to estimate, as explained below. Thus, the sample size needed to justify the statistical results, since these are large sample properties, increases with the number of categories, J, as well as the number of independent variables, K. Instances in which $K(J-1)$ exceed about 50 are pushing the limits of practicality.

As before, let $N_i$ indicate the number of replications or observations on the dependent variable Y in cell i, and let $N_{ji}$ represent the number of observations out of the $N_i$ for which Y takes on the value j, j = 1, ..., J. Then, $N_i = \sum_j N_{j,i}$.

The multinomial logistic probabilities are given by:

$$P_{ji} \equiv P(Y = j \,|\, X_i) = \exp[b_j' X_i]/D_i \qquad [4.13]$$

where

$$D_i = \sum_{j=1}^{J} [\exp(b_j' X_i)] \qquad [4.14]$$

and $b'_j X_i$ represents $\Sigma b_{kj} X_{ik}$. The unknown parameters to estimate are, of course, the coefficients, $b_j$. Note that there are J sets of parameters in the model and that each set contains K coefficients. As explained in Chapter 2, not all of these sets of coefficients can be estimated. Rather, only J – 1 of them can be (as is also true in the dichotomous case, J = 2, since there we estimate one such set). By convention, $b_J$ is set to 0.[43] The remaining J – 1 sets are to be estimated.

The assumptions of multinomial logit are:

1. There are M observations on K exogenous variables. (These observations are termed "cells.") One of the K variables usually will be the constant 1 (to estimate an intercept term). Further, the K exogenous variables are not linearly dependent (hence requiring that M be at least as large as K).

2. The dependent variable is measured as the number of responses within each cell that fall into each of the J possible categories, where J is a positive integer greater than one.

3. The responses (replications) on Y are independent both within and across cells.

4. For a given observation on $X_i$, the probability that a response Y will be in category j is given by equation 4.13.

### 4.2.1 MAXIMUM LIKELIHOOD ESTIMATION

The extension of maximum likelihood estimation as described in Chapter 3 for the dichotomous case to this polytomous case is straightforward. Further, the method applies equally as well to replicated as to unreplicated data. The likelihood function is given by:

$$L(Y|X,B) = \prod_{i=1}^{M} \prod_{j=1}^{J} \left[ \frac{\exp(b'_j X_i)}{\sum\limits_{h=1}^{J} \exp(b'_h X_i)} \right]^{N_{ji}} \qquad [4.15]$$

where $B$ denotes all $K(J-1)$ coefficients to be estimated. Note that when the data are unreplicated ($N_{ji}$ is 0 or 1 for all i and j) and J = 2, this equation is identical to equation 3.4. The MLEs, therefore, are the values of $B$ which maximize expression 4.15, and they are found by the same sort of iterative algorithm as in the dichotomous case.

Section 2.5.2 discussed interpretation of the coefficients of the multinomial logit model. Methods of inference using maximum likelihood estimates proceeds as for the dichotomous case discussed in Chapter 3. One important difference between the dichotomous case and the polytomous case concerns hypothesis tests of a particular variable's impact on Y. In the dichotomous case, variable $X_k$ has no (statistically significant) effect on Y if its coefficient, $b_k$, is not significantly different from 0 (say, as revealed by the z- or t-test). In the polytomous case, there are $J-1$ coefficients associated with each exogenous variable. Therefore, the variable $X_k$ has no effect on Y only if all $J-1$ coefficients are simultaneoulsy 0. Therefore, the appropriate hypothesis test is a joint test on the $J-1$ coefficients, which can be done using either procedure described in Chapter 3.

### 4.2.2 AN EXAMPLE

Table 4.2 contains estimates of multinomial logit for the by now familiar test data of Table 1, Chapter 1. We used these data above in the dichotomous case. In that case, since students received either of three grades, A, B, or C, we collapsed the data to the dichotomy A versus (B or C). Here, we return to the original trichotomy. While grades are ordinal, we assume that they are only nominal for purposes of illustration. To emphasize the point, we assigned values of 1 for a C grade, 2 for an A, and 3 for a B.[44]

As before, the results in the table are a nearly verbatim reproduction of the program output. The three independent variables are the student's entering GPA, score on the TUCE pretest, and the PSI dummy variable indicating teaching method. Thus, $K = 4$, including the constant. Since $J-1$ equals 2 in this case, there are estimates for two coefficients for each independent variable (and the constant), and each coefficient has a standard error and t-ratio associated with it.

The results are, of course, quite close to those obtained in the various earlier estimations, though the sample size is a bit small to put too much reliance on the statistical properties of the estimates. The first GPA coefficient, $b_{2,1}$, is $-2.75$, indicating that a student becomes less likely to earn a C ($j = 1$) than a B ($j = 3$, the default option) as GPA increases. The positive coefficient estimate for $b_{2,2}$ ($2.107$) indicates that the chances of earning an A increase, relative to receiving a B, as GPA increases. Note that both of the t-ratios for the GPA coefficients are below the critical value of t, even at a 90 percent significance level. Yet, the chi-square statistic for the joint impact of GPA on course grade is $6.14$, well beyond the critical value at the 95 percent level. Thus, the joint test implies that, while neither coefficient is significantly different from 0, they differ from each other significantly. Therefore, we would conclude that GPA is significantly related to the dependent variable. As before, TUCE does not seem important in predicting the course grade. Note that *both* PSI coefficients are positive, indicating that taking the new teaching format

## TABLE 4.2
### Trichotomous Logit Analysis on PSI Data

Logit Analysis, 32 Observations, 3 Independent Variables, 3 Groups

| Variable Means by Group | | Group | | |
| --- | --- | --- | --- | --- |
| | 1 | 2 | 3 | Overall |
| Number Observations | 8 | 11 | 13 | 32 |
| 1 GPA | 2.7438 | 3.4327 | 3.0800 | 3.1172 |
| 2 TUCE | 20.750 | 23.545 | 21.308 | 21.937 |
| 3 PSI | 0.375 | 0.7272 | 0.2307 | 0.4375 |

| Final Logit Coefficients | Alternative | |
| --- | --- | --- |
| | 1 | 2 |
| 0 Constant | 6.778 | −10.61 |
| 1 GPA | −2.751 | 2.107 |
| 2 TUCE | 0.0317 | 0.106 |
| 3 PSI | 0.2393 | 2.426 |

| Asymptotic Standard Errors | Alternative | |
| --- | --- | --- |
| | 1 | 2 |
| 0 Constant | 5.012 | 5.121 |
| 1 GPA | 1.704 | 1.355 |
| 2 TUCE | 0.135 | 0.146 |
| 3 PSI | 1.122 | 1.090 |

| Asymptotic T Ratios | Alternative | |
| --- | --- | --- |
| | 1 | 2 |
| 0 Constant | 1.352 | −2.071 |
| 1 GPA | −1.614 | 1.555 |
| 2 TUCE | 0.2339 | 0.7258 |
| 3 PSI | 0.2133 | 2.226 |

| Variance-Coveriance Matrix | | | | (Variable, Alternative) | | | | |
| --- | --- | --- | --- | --- | --- | --- | --- | --- |
| | (0,1) | (0,2) | (1,1) | (1,2) | (2,1) | (2,2) | (2,1) | (3,2) |
| (0,1) | 25.12 | | | | | | | |
| (0,2) | 3.970 | 26.23 | | | | | | |
| (1,1) | −7.156 | −0.9934 | 2.903 | | | | | |
| (1,2) | −0.8129 | −5.170 | 0.4196 | 1.836 | | | | |
| (2,1) | −0.1957 | −0.0395 | −0.0620 | −0.0226 | 0.0183 | | | |
| (2,2) | −0.0623 | −0.3430 | −0.0151 | −0.0463 | 0.0051 | 0.0213 | | |
| (3,1) | −1.011 | 0.2460 | 0.3841 | −0.1078 | −0.0210 | 0.0029 | 1.259 | |
| (3,2) | −0.4224 | −2.208 | 0.1159 | 0.3667 | 0.0006 | 0.0180 | 0.3146 | 1.189 |

−2 Log Likelihood     49.57

Chi-Square Test for Independent Variables, 2 Degrees of Freedom

GPA     6.14          TUCE   0.53          PSI     5.09

Overall Chi-Square, 6 Degrees of Freedom   19.52

makes it more likely to earn either a C or an A. However, the first PSI variable's coefficient is very small and not significantly different from 0, while the A versus B comparison is larger and significant.

### 4.2.3 MINIMUM CHI-SQUARE ESTIMATION OF THE POLYTOMOUS LOGIT MODEL

If the data are replicated and there is a large number of replications in each of the M cells, then an extension of the Minimum Chi-Square or WLS estimator described in section 4.1 may be used. As before, the "true" logits are logarithms of the odds ratio, except that there are $J-1$ of them:[45]

$$\log[P(Y = j)/P(Y = J)] = b'_j X_i \qquad \text{for } j = 1, \ldots, J-1 \qquad [4.16]$$

The $j$ proportions or relative frequencies of responses are:

$$P_{ji} = N_{ji}/N_i \qquad j = 1, \ldots, J; \ i = 1, \ldots, M \qquad [4.17]$$

and these can be used to compute the "observed" logits:

$$L_{ji} = \log[p_{ji}/p_J] \qquad j = 1, \ldots, J-1; \ i = 1, \ldots, M \qquad [4.18]$$

These $J-1$ observed logits, then, serve as the dependent variables in the $J-1$ regression equations,

$$L_{ji} = b'_j X_i + u_{ji} \qquad \text{for } j = 1, \ldots, J-1 \qquad [4.19]$$

where the $u_{ji}$ represent the error, i.e., the difference between the "true" and observed logits (equation 4.18 minus equation 4.16).

OLS estimates of the $J-1$ equations, 4.19, yield unbiased but inefficient parameter estimates. One could use the standard WLS weighting procedure. However, there is also a correlation of error terms between $u_{ji}$ and $u_{j'i}$ for all $j, j' = 1, \ldots, J-1$. The reason for the later correlation is that the $J-1$ observed logits are based on the $J$ response proportions, and these must sum to one by definition. Therefore, if one $p_{ji}$ is "large," then the other $p_{ji}$s must be "small." In turn, "abnormally" large values of an observed logit, $L_{ji}$ must be compensated for by other "abnormally" small values of $L_{j'i}$. An estimation procedure that takes this correlation into account is using more information, and it will yield estimates with better sampling properties. The procedure for correcting for heteroscedasticity and for correlation across logits is complicated. The interested reader is referred to Amemiya (1981: 1515).

## 5. SUMMARY AND EXTENSIONS

### 5.0 Introduction

We have two tasks in this chapter. The first is to review and emphasize the highlights of material covered in the preceding four chapters. The second is to give the reader some sense of extensions that are possible and relationships of these techniques to others. There are many other aspects to qualitative data analysis within the basic framework of the general linear model, and indeed many of them are limitations on what one can do with such techniques as probit, logit or the LPM in comparison to the Gauss-Markov, OLS regression approach. Further, there are many "special topics," relationships among various techniques, and so on, which should be brought to the attention of the reader.

### 5.1 Summary

The purpose of this summary is to emphasize the points we feel are most important and deserving of reiteration.

The first is that the techniques covered in this volume are all variations of the standard linear framework. That is, they can be seen as extensions of the general linear model, since all rest on a linear relationship between Y and X in some form, albeit often with some nonlinear transformation. That is, the fundamental assumption for all of these techniques, including OLS, is that the mean of Y is given by $F(b'X_i)$. The models differ in their choice of F. For the linear probability model, F is an identity. For probit or logit, F is a particular nonlinear transformation. The really important point, then, is that these techniques preserve as many of the great strengths of the linear model as possible, including the ease with which useful and interesting inferences can be drawn from the data.

The second point is that the ordinary regression approach is not being followed for a reason. The reason is that some of the conditions required by the Gauss-Markov assumptions cannot be maintained and others are implausible in the class of cases considered here. We are examining situations in which the endogenous or dependent variable, $Y_i$, is measured as a dichotomy or as a polytomy. As a consequence of the discrete nature of $Y_i$, the distribution of the random component of the regression equation cannot be independent of the "indepedent" variables, thus making the full set of Gauss-Markov assumptions untenable. It then follows that many of the formal conclusions that underlie inference with ordinary regression cannot be demonstrated. Even worse, we can—

and did—show examples in which they fail. Thus, in general, OLS regression estimates with a dichotomous endogenous variable are not BLUE. In fact, they can be quite misleading and in particular are sensitive to the particular range of observations on $X_i$ in the sample. Finally, estimates of coefficient parameters are constrained artificially, by the imposition of the OLS assumptions (or their equivalent) where they are not warranted.

In sum, ordinary least squares estimates with a limited endogenous variable, $Y_i$, have few desirable and many undesirable properties. The problem is that assumptions are imposed that one knows in advance cannot be maintained. In short, the regression user, in this case, knowingly misspecifies the relationship between $Y_i$ and $X_i$.

The usual answer to the misspecification problem is to specify the model correctly. While one rarely knows the "true" specification, every attempt should be made to choose a specification that is plausible in place of one that is implausible. And, of course, that is just what we did.

There are an infinite number of possible specifications of the relationship between $Y_i$ and $X_i$. The linear is one of them, and the linear probability model (LPM) is a specification that preserves linearity while acknowledging the more blatant of the erroneous Gauss-Markov assumptions.

Nonlinear specifications abound, and there are reasons to believe that they are more plausible in many cases with limited dependent variables than is the linear assumption. We provided a number of possible nonlinear specifications but pointed out that only two of them, probit and logit, have received much attention. That is, estimation procedures have been derived for these two techniques and their statistical properties investigated. Thus, they can be used to make meaningful and helpful inferences, much like the simplest OLS regression cases.

Probit and logit (or the other possible nonlinear specifications) are arbitrary. But, in comparison to the equally arbitrary linear model (with Gauss-Markov assumptions), we do not know for sure that they are wrong. (Of course, if we do know they are wrong in a particular situation, we should no more use them than we should use any other incorrect statistical technique.)

The assumptions that underlie either probit or logit, beyond that specifying the relation between the mean of Y and $X$, are really quite similar to, and no more restrictive than, the remaining Gauss-Markov assumptions in OLS regression. Thus, the use of probit or logit is no more restrictive than is OLS in the general linear model.

Moreover, the set of inferences about parameter estimates that can be made with either nonlinear technique is virtually identical to that of OLS regression, with one qualifier and one exception. The qualification is that all properties hold only as approximations in large samples. This caveat applies to most applications of OLS to the general linear model, too, although it is seldom acknowledged. Still, it appears that probit and logit require larger samples than the standard regression model for the approximations to be adequate. The exception is that there is no ready equivalent to the coefficient of determination ($R^2$). We proposed, hesitantly, a number of possible alternatives, but all suffer from a lack of wide acceptance, and none has an interpretaion as simple as the regression $R^2$.

With properties known, statistical inferences and hypothesis tests can be conducted in a fashion quite like that with regression in the general linear model, though interpretation of the inferences of most direct interest is somewhat more difficult for probit, logit, or any nonlinear technique. One can easily test, for example, whether the impact of, say, $X_1$ on Y is statistically significant. However, assessing the magnitude of the impact is a bit more complicated than in linear regression. As opposed to linear regression, the impact of, say, a unit change in $X_1$ on Y depends on more than just the coefficient value. Rather, it also depends upon what the particular value of $X_1$ is—and on what the particular observations are on all other exogenous variables. In short, with a linear relationship, the impact of a unit change is a constant equal to the slope parameter. In a nonlinear relationship, it matters just where you are on the curve. Still, general assessments of the relative impact of variables are possible.

These, then, are the basic conclusions of what we have done at this point. The obvious remaining question is whether one should use logit, probit, or the LPM. The best way to answer this question is to see what we did not cover in this paper. Before doing so, however, we should note two things. First, all three techniques yield estimates that have quite similar properties (e.g., asymptotically unbiased, efficient and normal), so that there is little to gain from one technique over another in terms of inferences that can be made. Second, the LPM differs from probit and logit in being linear, so that the linearity assumption may be the key to that choice. However, probit and logit, while being different nonlinear transformations, yield results that are essentially indistinguishable from each other, so that there is very little here to guide choice of one over the other. Potential extensions can help some.

## 5.2 Extensions

### 5.2.1 VIOLATIONS OF ASSUMPTIONS

What we have covered here is analogous to the material of approximately the first half of a course on least squares regression. The second broad topic is what to do if the Gauss-Markov assumptions fail, and related problems.

Here, there has been little work done with any of the three techniques covered. One could reason by analogy that underspecification leads to biased estimates, that first-order serial correlation affects efficiency, and so on. The analogies are hard to verify because of the nonlinearity of the estimation procedure. While many questions remain unanswered, some analytic results have been obtained, and Monte Carlo studies have provided additional insight. Using analytic methods on closely related models, Robinson (1982) has shown that, when the residuals are serially correlated, maximum likelihood estimates remain unbiased in large samples, but they are not efficient. This result is precisely analogous to that of autocorrelated linear models. Unfortunately, corrections for serial correlation have proven untractable in the logit and probit cases.

One important use of the Monte Carlo method has been to investigate how large a sample one needs before estimates converge "close enough" to make use of the asymptotic properties. The answer depends upon the number of variables, the degree of their covariation, and so forth, but for most applications, the rule of thumb of 50 cases per parameter seem safe.

Recently, econometricians have turned their attention to one of the most vexing limitations of these techniques. The specification assumption includes (implicitly, if not explicitly) the assumption that Y is the only endogenous variable in the "system." In reality, of course, any reasonably rich theory of any social process includes some set of equations and, therefore, more than one endogenous variable. And one of the major topics in econometrics is to investigate just how best to estimate sets of equations.

In the linear model, if the system of equations is purely recursive, then the equations can be arranged "triangularly" and, if no other assumptions are violated, estimated without loss of properties by OLS. In the cases considered here, the same is true, and probit, logit, or the LPM can be substituted for OLS where appropriate.

Of more interest are "pseudo-recursive" systems (i.e., a recursive structure but with nonindependent errors) and nonrecursive systems (in which, let us say, $Y_1$ affects Y and $Y_2$ affects $Y_1$ in the same time period). In least squares regression, some instrumental-variable technique (e.g., two-stage least squares) or some system-method (e.g., three-stage least squares) is required to assure desirable statistical properties and justifiable inferences. Only recently has much progress been made in the case of limited dependent variable estimation techniques. One solution is a method analogous to two stage least squares. Since they are not yet incorporated in many probit and logit routines (and since this area is rapidly developing), we only refer you to the current literature (Heckman [1978], Nelson and Olson [1978], and Amemiya [1978]). Actual use of such procedures requires more statistical and programming skills than we assume the average reader of this paper possesses.

### 5.2.2 CONNECTIONS WITH OTHER TECHNIQUES

Logit models bear a close association to other statistical techniques. For example, the choice probabilities explicit in logit can be derived from the structure of the discriminant analysis model (Klecka, 1980). Discriminant analysis can be thought of as treating the endogenous variable in logit as the independent variable and asking, given Y, how is the distribution of the X's best described (in effect treating the X's as "endogenous" variables).

Similarly, logit is mathematically related to log-linear models (Knoke and Burke, 1980). This similarity should not be too surprising, as logit, like log-linear models, assumes that the log-odds ratio of Y is linearly related to the independent variables. The difference between the two models is that log-linear models focus on the joint outcome probabilities of a set of qualitative variables, while logit examines the conditional probability of a single qualitative variable, given a set of other variables (which may be qualitative or cardinal).

While the logit model is closely related to other statistical methods, the probit model has been extended to cover a wide variety of qualitative and limited dependent variables. In one very natural extension, McKelvey and Zavoina (1976) extend the probit model to cover the case of an ordinal dependent variable. Tobin (1958), in one of the earliest extensions of probit, initiated investigation of a class of models in which the dependent variable is interval but limited in range (i.e., takes on a wide range of values, like a standard interval variable, but also takes on discrete points as well). For example, expenditures on durable goods may take on a wide range of positive values, but it may also take on the particular value of zero very often (the value zero is referred to as a "mass point" since it occurs much too frequently to be considered just another of the infinitely many values that the variable "expenditures" may take on). Tobin's model (dubbed "Tobit" by Goldberger [1964]) involves one limit, either a maximum or minimum. Rossett (1959) proposed a "friction model" with a mass point in the center of a range of continuous values, while Rossett and Nelson (1975) examined a Tobit-like model with two limits, one a maximum, the other a minimum. Amemiya (1984) surveys these sorts of models, while Maddala (1983) provides a comprehensive treatment of these and of qualitative variable methods.

Finally, a straight-forward extension of the qualitative variable models discussed here is to allow for exogenous variables that describe the alternative in the choice set, as opposed to describing the agent making the choice as our discussion has implicitly assumed throughout. For example, one might be interested in a model of voting behavior in senatorial primary elections. The independent variables might be descriptions of the candidates, incumbency, committee assignments, campaign budgets, and the like, while the dependent variable is the share of the vote for each candidate. The candidates running in each election will of course differ across states and even the number of candidates in each primary election (observation) may differ. A statistical model which describes such a setting has been called the "conditional logit model." The interested reader is referred to McFadden (1974).

The only real conclusion, then, is that the choice of estimation procedure should be based on the theoretical questions first and foremost, based secondly on assumptions one can reasonably hope to be close approximations of the way the data on hand were generated, and thirdly, on the ability of the technique to make possible inferences of interest. The failure of a statistical technique to satisfy any of the three criteria renders it unsuitable for use. We hope that the reader has gained a better appreciation of a set of techniques that are often going to be better approximations for estimation in one of the most commonly encountered situations in the social sciences, when the dependent variable is qualitative.

# NOTES

1. Actually, "exogenous" and "independent" variables are not exactly the same. An independent variable, as its name suggests, is one that is not explained by the regression model in any way. Exogenous variables include independent variables, but also can include temporally prior values of dependent variables. The distinction becomes particularly important when dealing with systems of dynamic equations. In a single equation model, especially one with cross-sectional data, the distinction is less crucial. Since we will be confining our attention to single equations we shall, somewhat inaccurately, use these two terms as synonyms. The correct term is "exogenous," but "independent" is the more common usage.

2. To avoid cumbersome notation, we shall not give the full notation to summation signs unless there is a possibility of confusion. Instead, we use either just the summation sign itself or the summation sign topped by K (when summing over variables) or N (when summing over observations). Thus 1.1 may be written:

$$Y_i = \sum_{i=1}^{K} b_k X_{ik} + u_i$$

or

$$Y_i = \sum^{K} b_k X_{ik} + u_i$$

3. Typically one of the $X_{ik}$, say the first, is fixed at 1 for all observations. Its coefficient, $b_1$, is then interpreted as the intercept term and the other $b_k$s are "slope" coefficients.

4. "Least squares" follows from minimization of the sum of squared errors. The qualifier "ordinary" refers to the linearity, in the $b_k$, of the "error" defined by 1.3 and the fact that its square is unweighed in the sum, thus distinguishing it from "nonlinear least squares," "weighted least squares," "generalized least squares," and so on.

5. Since $u_i$ is a theoretical "error" term and $e_i$ an estimated one, we shall refer to $u_i$ as the disturbance term and $e_i$ the error term.

6. Note that if $X_{i1}$ is the constant 1, it too is multiplied by $w_i$. Therefore, the second stage regression must be run *without* an intercept term, that is $w_i$ is to replace the intercept. Unfortunately, many computer programs do not allow for the deletion of the intercept, although this option is becoming more common (having been added to SPSS, for example). Also, note that the $w_i$'s obtained from the first stage regression are estimates (being based on $\hat{b}_k$, rather than $b_k$). In moderate sized samples, say less than 100, some caution should be exercised in too strong a reliance on the results. Finally, note that in principle, a third, or fourth, or, etc., round of reestimations of $w_i$ could be followed, but such practice seems to make little difference and there is no theoretical work to show that the succeeding estimates would be better.

7. The procedure described employs only OLS routines with some facility for transforming variables. Many canned programs provide for weighted least square analysis and require only a definition of the weight to be used. While the computational ease of such routines is obvious, some care needs to be exercised in their use. Different programs use various definitions of the weight. Some ask for the reciprocal of the variable w defined

above. Others ask for its square. An example of the latter is the widely used SAS package. This is the one employed for the results reported here.

8. As estimates of a probability, therefore, they are nonsensical. Note, too, that an estimate of exactly 0 or exactly 1 is problematic, for the resultant weight, $w_i$, will be undefined (the denominator of equation 1.8 will be zero). Five observations in the example of the last section were estimated to be outside the 0-1 range. They were truncated in ways described below.

9. Even after truncating the negative scores to .001, the *second* stage of the procedure yielded negative probabilities (albeit very nearly zero). Note that the argument was not that the LPM assumption, per se, was incorrect, but that the model as a whole was not correctly specified.

10. In particular, the variance $u_j$, $V(u_j)$ would be:

$$V(u_j) = (\Sigma b_k X_{jk}) (1 - \Sigma b_k X_{jk})/N_j$$

11. As in section 1.2, problems arise if any of the $f_j$ happen to be exactly 0 or 1. The practical solution is, once again, to truncate $f_j$ to, say, .01 or .99.

12. We investigate here the case of a dependent variable measured in nominal categories. An intermediate step between the nominal and interval level is the ordinal variable. Since ordinality provides more information than nominal measures, it is not surprising that there are stronger techniques for that case than those considered here. One relevant instance is provided by McKelvey and Zavoina (1976), who extend probit from the dichotomous to the case of n-ordinal categories.

13. The disturbance terms, $u_{ij}$, will ordinarily be correlated across the equations. This correlation presents no problems in estimation, as it violates no assumption. In fact, the cross-equation of $u_{ij}$'s provides more information that can be used to achieve even more efficient estimates. This procedure is known as "seemingly unrelated regressions" and can be found in Kmenta (1971) and elsewhere.

14. Actually, there is a third crucial aspect of specification: that Y is, in fact, dependent on the X's, while the X's are not, in turn, dependent on Y; that is, each $X_k$ variable is independent the disturbance term. Many of the most interesting problems in dealing with sets of simultaneous equations concern this aspect of specification. We are assuming here, of course, that Y can be described accurately by a single equation and that Y does not affect the values of any of the X variables simultaneously.

15. We are explicitly ruling out the possibility that $P_i$ equals one or zero exactly. Outcomes are viewed as never being certain. There is some probability, perhaps arbitrarily close to zero, that a presidential candidate will vote for his opponent.

16. This model can be defined formally as:

$$F(Z) = \begin{cases} 1 & \text{if } 1 \leqslant Z \\ Z & \text{if } 0 < Z < 1 \\ 0 & \text{if } Z \leqslant 0 \end{cases}$$

17. The formal definition is:

$$F(Z) = \begin{cases} 1 & \text{if } \pi/2 \leqslant Z \\ [1 + \sin(Z)]/2 & \text{if } -\pi/2 < Z < \pi/2 \\ 0 & \text{if } Z \leqslant -\pi/2 \end{cases}$$

18. The equation for the Gompertz curve is:

$$F(Z) = \exp\left[-\exp\left(-Z\right)\right]$$

19. The formal definition is:

$$F(Z) = \begin{cases} 1 - (1+Z)^{-C} & 0 \leqslant Z \\ 0 & Z < 0 \end{cases}$$

where C is a parameter to be chosen or estimated. If $C = 1$, there is a close relationship between this and the logistic curve discussed below. In particular the Z here equals $\exp(z)$ where z is the ordinate of the logistic curve. The parameter C allows for asymmetries. If $C = 1$, the curve is symmetric about $Z = 1$ (or $z = \log Z = 0$). If $C > 1$, the curve is skewed left, while if $C < 1$, the curve is skewed right. This flexibility is attractive, but C turns out to be difficult to estimate with any precision. That Z must be greater than zero can raise troubles under the specification $Z_i = b_k X_{ik}$. Even if all $X_{ik}$'s are positive, either all $b_k$'s must be positive (or zero), or complicated restrictions must be imposed. We could specify alternatively that $\log(Z_i) = \Sigma b_k \log(X_{ik})$ (or $Z_i = \Pi X_{ik}^{b_k}$), but, with $C = 1$, that would be identical to the logistic curve, with the ordinate $z_i = \log Z_i$ and all exogenous variables expressed in logarithmic form.

20.    The formal definition of Urban's curve is:

$$F(Z) = \frac{1}{2} + \frac{1}{\pi} \tan^{-2}(Z)$$

The other two are important enough that their formulas are in the text.

21. The $W_i$ terms (and the $Y_i^*$ to be defined below) are interval level variables which are not observed and measured and, indeed, may be inherently unobservable. $W_i$ may have any number of interpretations, utility, expected gain or profit, etc., depending upon the particular application.

22. We follow convention and ease in later manipulations in defining $u_i$ as $v_{i2} - v_{i1}$. This makes the negative of $u_i$ appear in equation 2.8b, but since this disturbance term is not observable it makes no difference which way we define it. Changing its sign would merely make the algebra more cumbersome.

23. For example, if $u_i$ is distributed as a Cauchy random variable, we obtain Urban's curve, and if $u_i$ is uniformally distributed over some interval, say $(a, b)$, we obtain the truncated linear probability model that is 0 to the point $Z = a$, increases linearly to the point $Z = b$ (where $f(Z) = 1$), and is constantly 1 thereafter. (As a result, the linear probability model is derivable from equation 2.8b and the assumption that $u_i$ is "diffusely uniform," i.e., uniformly distributed over the interval $(-\infty, \infty)$.)

24. To see that 2.13 and 2.14 are the same as 2.15, consider the denominator:

$$\left[ 1 + \sum_{j=1}^{J-1} \exp(Z_{ij}) \right]$$

Since $b_{Jk}$ are defined as zero and since $\exp(0) = 1$, this can be written as

$$\left[ \exp(Z_{iJ}) + \sum_{j=1}^{J-1} \exp(Z_{ij}) \right] \quad \text{or} \quad \left[ \sum_{j=1}^{J} \exp(Z_{ij}) \right]$$

where $Z_{ij} = 0$ if $j = J$. Thus, setting $b_{Jk} = 0$ provides an (abritary but fully general) normalization for solving the $J - 1$ equations in $J - 1$ unknowns (the $Z_j$). Recall that $Z_{ij} = \Sigma b_{jk}X_{ik}$.

25. McKelvey and Zavoina (1976) deal with probit for *ordinal*, multi-category dependent variables.

26. The use of calculus assumes the $X_k$ in question is strictly continuous. If this assumption is not valid at least approximately, for example if $X_k$ is a dummy variable which assumes only the values zero and one, it may be better to compute the effect directly as

$$dP/dX_k = P(Y = 1 | X, X_k = 1) - P(Y = 1 | X, X_k = 0)$$

27. Note that one of the X variables will be assumed to be the number 1 representing a constant term. By convention, that variable is $X_1$. Thus, there are $K - 1$ exogenous variables, from variable $X_2$ through variable $X_k$. In some programs, the user is required to input the constant term by inclusion of a "variable" that is a string of N ones, one for each of the N cases.

28. OLS estimation of the standard linear regression model is shown to yield exactly the same estimates as application of the method of MLE when the disturbances follow a normal distribution. Thus, the two are interchangeable in the standard case, and texts focus on OLS because it is a bit simpler conceptually. It is possible to derive estimates of the probit and logit models by least squares methods. However, in these cases the least squares estimator is not linear (and thus not "ordinary") and also inefficient. The weighted least squares alternative is efficient, but it too is nonlinear. Moreover, the weighted nonlinear least squares estimator for probit and logit models with unreplicated data turns out to be identical to the MLE estimator. Thus the text follows the more common maximum likelihood derivation.

29. Starting from an initial "guess" of the coefficient values $b$, a solution algorithm determines the direction and size of a change in $b$ which will increase the objective function (in this case the log of the likelihood). The coefficients are changed by this amount and the process repeats in an iterative fashion. When no further change will produce a sufficient improvement in the objective (increase in the likelihood) the procedure stops (the algorithm is said to converge). A number of different convergence criteria (measures of "sufficient improvement") can be employed, such as the (percentage) change in the objective or the (percentage) change in the coefficients. Different algorithms use different means of computing the change, from one iteration to the next, in the coefficients. The algorithm most frequently employed for probit and logit problems is "Newton-Raephson." The matrix formula it uses for changing the coefficients is

$$b^{(i+1)} = b^{(i)} - H^{-1}g$$

where the superscript on $b$ indicates the iteration number, g (the "gradient") is the vector of the first derivatives of the likelihood function and H (the "hessian") is the matrix of second derivatives. Note that when convergence is achieved, g should be 0, so that closeness of g to 0 serves as an alternative convergence criterion. Probit and logit likelihood functions are sufficiently smooth that (a) there is guaranteed to be a unique solution to the maximization problem and (b) an alogrithm such as Newton-Raephson seldom takes more than 6-10 iterations to converge even when the initial coefficient guess is a poor one. (Failure to converge within this number may be an indication of "multicolinearity." Of course other algorithms may take longer even on well behaved problems.) Note that the negative inverse of the hessian matrix $(-H^{-1})$ is the appropriate estimate of the covariance matrix of the coefficients $b$.

30. $s_{jk}$ represents the estimated covariance between $b_j$ and $b_k$. Therefore, $s_{jk} = s_{kj}$. Since the variance-covariance matrix is symmetric, some programs report only the lower (bottom left) or upper (top right) triangle of off-diagonal terms. A diagonal element of this matrix, $s_{kk}$, is the variance of the coefficient $b_k$, and its square root is the standard error of the coefficient, denoted $s_k$ above. One can compute the correlation between two coefficients, say $r_{jk}$ (analogous to the Pearson's product moment correlation) by the formula $r_{jk} = s_{jk}/s_j s_k$ (the covariance divided by the product of the two standard errors). Since correlations are easier to interpret than covariances, some programs may allow for the output of the matrix of correlations among coefficient estimates rather than, or in addition to, the covariance matrix.

31. The likelihood ratio test is a very general one for testing nested hypotheses in the context of maximum likelihood estimation. The general form of the statistic is simply to take the negative of twice the natural logarithm of the ratio of the two likelihood values:

$$c = -2(\log[L0/L1])$$

L0 is the maximal value of the likelihood function when the constraints implied by the null hypothesis are in force (e.g., that all coefficients but the constant are zero), and L1 is the maximal value under the alternative hypothesis (i.e., the likelihood function as estimated without the hypothesized constraints). If the model implied by the null hypothesis is nested within (i.e., a special case of) the model associated with the alternative hypothesis (e.g., certain coefficients are 0 is a special case of a model with no constraints on any coefficients), then the statistic c will follow approximately a chi-square distribution with the degrees of freedom determined by the number of constraints imposed in the null hypothesis $(K-1$ for the case of the standard null hypothesis for testing goodness of fit).

32. The regression F-statistic can likewise be derived from the likelihood ratio principle, so it and the test proposed here are conceptually identical. (Recall that OLS and MLE are identical under the assumptions of the standard normal regression model.) Moreover, since an F-statistic times numerator degrees of freedom approaches a chi square as its denominator degrees of freedom grows large, the two statistics follow the same distribution in large samples (e.g., $N - K > 100$). The only differences between the two tests, then, are computational details and the fact that the exact small sample behavior of the statistic reported here has not been determined. Many practitioners treat the statistic c, divided by its degrees of freedom $(K-1)$, as an F statistic with $K-1$ and $N-K$ degrees of freedom. They do so in smaller samples, in particular, because it makes the test more conservative (the so called "asymptotic F").

33. It may not be obvious that this equation is the maximum likelihood value under the null hypothesis for either the probit or logit model. To see that it is so, note that, under the null, the probability that Y is one is a constant across all X values, and that therefore the maximum likelihood estimate of that probability is the observed proportion of responses of $Y-1$, namely $N1/N$. Substitution into either likelihood equation, for probit or logit, yields the expression above after taking logarithms. We could also solve for b, from $\Phi(b_1) = N1/N$ in the probit model or $\exp(b_1)/[1 + \exp(b_1)] = N1/N$ in the logit model

to obtain the estimate of the constant coefficient under the null hypothesis, but that estimate is generally less interesting than the likelihood itself.

34. Recall that if a random variable z follows a normal distribution with mean zero and variance v, then $(z'z)/v$ is a chi-square variable with one degree of freedom. The multivariate extension of this result is that if z follows a J-variate normal distribution with mean vector $0$ and covariance matrix $V$, then $z'V^{-1}z$ is a chi-square variate with J degrees of freedom. Thus the result above follows as a large sample approximation from the asymptotic normality of maximum likelihood estimates.

35. To see that the two tests are equivalent, recall that the square of a t with n degrees of freedom is an F with 1 and n degrees of freedom, and the latter converges to a chi-square distribution with one degree of freedom as n gets large. Alternatively, a t with n degrees of freedom converges to a normal with mean 0, variance 1 as n grows large, and the square of a normal $(0, 1)$ is a chi square with one degree of freedom. Thus, the only difference between the t-test described earlier and the chi-square test suggested here is a small sample correction for degrees of freedom in the t test. The analogous correction here would be to divide the c statistic by its degrees of freedom, J, and treat the result as an $F(J, N-K)$ variate. Finally, note that for a single coefficient the t test is preferred to the chi square since the former allows for either one or two tailed tests while the latter permits only a two-tailed test.

36. Some programs (e.g., the logit program used in estimating the results reported in Table 3.2) are written to solve for $P(Y = 0 | X)$. $P(Y = 1 | X)$ can be solved by the formula $(PY = 1) = 1 - P(Y = 0)$. Note that if the program is written to solve for $P(Y = 0)$, all signs on the coefficients will be reversed (including that of the constant). While, obviously, some care must be exercised to avoid reaching the exact opposite conclusions, it is also worth noting that all standard errors, covariances, goodness of fit measures and the like will be unaffected.

37. This procedure is ordinarily called "minimum chi square," as its initial derivation by Berkson (1944) was based on minimizing a chi-square value quite similar to the common chi-square statistic for testing independence in contingency tables. Theil (1972) introduced this estimation to the social sciences but derived it in the WLS fashion presented here. The estimator may also be called the Berkson-Theil WLS estimator.

38. Grouped data refers to situations in which the exogenous variables have been broken into categories and records kept only on the category in which an observation falls, not the actual level of the exogenous variable. With coarse enough categories or enough observations, the data can be placed as in a contingency table of manageable dimensions, and the methods proposed in this chapter might then be used for estimation. Such a setting is not recommended. The economies achieved are generally more than offset by the loss in information resulting from the grouping, and, worse, the grouping of the exogenous variables may cause problems of the sort commonly described by errors in variables.

39. Note from equation 4.4 that the observed logits will not be defined if $p_i$ equals either zero or one. So $N_i$ must be at least (and in practice much greater than) two for every i for the procedures discussed here to be applicable. Moreover, the statistical properties of the estimator described below depend on the quality of the sample proportions $p_i$ as estimates of the probabilities $P_i$. These in turn will be good estimates so long as the number of replications, $N_i$, is reasonably large. A standard rule of thumb is that in every cell both $N1_i$ and $N0_i$ should be at least five.

40. The proof of these three results follows easily using elementary calculus. Expand $L_i$ in a Taylor series about the point $P_i$, obtaining

$$L_i - \log\{P_i/[1 - P_i]\} = [p_i - P_i]/\{P_i[1 - P_i]\} + R$$

The term on the left is the error term $u_i$ whose properties we are investigating. We see that it behaves like $[p_i - P_i]$ divided by the constant $P_i[1 - P_i]$ plus some remainder term R. Since $p_i$ is the maximum likelihood estimator of $P_i$, it is consistent. So, for large $N_i$, R is negligible compared to the other term and may be neglected. Now $p_i N_i$ is binomial, so $p_i$ has a mean of $P_i$ and a variance of $P_i[1 - P_i]/N_i$. Thus we see that $u_i$ has a mean of zero and a variance of $1/\{N_i P_i[1 - P_i]\}$. Applying a central limit theorem, we see further that the limiting distribution of u is normal.

41. Note that the weight should be applied to the intercept term as well as all other exogenous variables. If the statistical software being employed does not handle the weighting automatically, and as always it is important to verify the correctness of the weighting used, this means that in the regression the intercept should be omitted and the square root of $N_i p_i[1 - p_i]$ should be included in its place as one of the regressors. The coefficient of this term is the intercept.

42. There is a potential for confusion on this issue with regard to degrees of freedom computations for various hypothesis tests. Since there are M "observations," canned regression programs will take the degrees of freedom to be $M - K$. But the real sample size is the total number of replications, not M, so $(\Sigma N_i) - K$ is a better and potentially quite different degree of freedom correction. Of course, there is no precise statistical justification for any particular correction since the only known statistical properties are large sample ones. As suggested earlier in connection with other estimators, if the degrees of freedom correction makes a difference in the outcome of the hypothesis tests as compared with using "infinity" degrees of freedom, the sample size is probably too small to justify the analysis.

43. As explained in Chapter 2, this particular normalization rule means that a coefficient set, say $b_j$, is to be interpreted as measuring the effect of the exogenous variables on the choice *between* Y = j and Y = J. Computer programs differ in the normalization rule they use. Many, for example, set $b_1$ instead of $b_J$, to 0. Since the labeling of Y is arbitrary, one could change the particular interpretation of coefficients simply by relabeling Y values. Further, estimated values can be renormalized easily to any base. For example, obtaining new coefficient values, $b_j^* = b_j - b_2$ for all j, yields new coefficients normalized to Y = 2. The only difficulty is that standard errors and some hypothesis tests refer to the normalization employed at estimation and not to the renormalized coefficients.

44. The fact that A, B, and C have a natural order is irrelevant here. Multinomial logit neither imposes ordinal constraints, nor makes use of such information. If the dependent variable is truly ordinal, procedures such as McKelvey and Zavoina's (1976) ordinal probit model would be more appropriate.

45. The denominator of the odds ratio is the probability of the $J^{th}$ response. Any other denominator would serve equally as well. However, whatever is used determines the normalization (here, that $b_J = 0$).

# REFERENCES

ABRAMSON, P. R., J. H. ALDRICH, and D. W. ROHDE (1983) Change and Continuity in the 1980 Elections. Washington, DC: Congressional Quarterly Press.

ACHEN, C. H. (1982) Interpreting and Using Regression. Sage University Papers: Quantitative Applications in the Social Sciences, 07-029. Beverly Hills, CA: Sage.

AMEMIYA, T. (1984) "Tobit models." Journal of Econometrics, forthcoming.

――――(1981) "Qualitative response models: a survey." Journal of Economic Literature 19: 1483-1536.

――――(1978) "The estimation of a simultaneous equation generalized probit model." Econometrica 46: 1193-1205.

BERKSON, J. (1944) "Application of the logistic function to bio-assay." Journal of the American Statistical Association 39: 357-365.

FINNEY, D. J. (1971) Probit Analysis. Cambridge: Cambridge University Press. (Originally published 1947.)

GOLDBERGER, A. S. (1964) Econometric Theory. New York: John Wiley.

HECKMAN, J. J. (1978) "Dummy endogenous variables in a simultaneous equation system." Econometrica 46: 931-960.

JOHNSTON, J. (1984) Econometric Methods. New York: McGraw-Hill.

KLECKA, W. R. (1980) Discriminant Analysis. Sage University Papers: Quantitative Applications in the Social Sciences, 07-019. Beverly Hills, CA: Sage.

KMENTA, J. (1971) Elements of Econometrics. New York: Macmillan.

KNOKE, D. and P. J. BURKE (1980) Log-Linear Models. Sage University Papers: Quantitative Applications in the Social Sciences, 07-020. Beverly Hills, CA: Sage.

LEWIS-BECK, M. S. (1980) Applied Regression: An Introduction. Sage University Papers: Quantitative Applications in the Social Sciences, 07-022. Beverly Hills, CA: Sage.

LUCE, R. D. and P. SUPPES (1965) "Preference, utility, and subjective probability," in R. D. Luce, R. Bush, and E. Galanter (eds.) Handbook of Mathematical Psychology, Vol. 3. New York: John Wiley.

MADDALA, G. S. (1983) Limited-Dependent and Qualitative Variables in Econometrics. Cambridge: Cambridge University Press.

McFADDEN, D. (1973) "Conditional logit analysis of qualitative choice behavior," in P. Zarembka (ed.) Frontiers in Econometrics. New York: Academic Press.

McKELVEY, R. D. and W. ZAVOINA (1976) "A statistical model for the analysis of ordinal level dependent variables." Journal of Mathematical Sociology 4: 103-120.

NELSON, F. D. and L. OLSON (1978) "Specification and estimation of a simultaneous-equation model with limited dependent variables." International Economic Review 19: 695-709.

OSTROM, C. W., Jr. and J. H. ALDRICH (1978) "The relationship between size and stability in the major power international system." American Journal of Political Science 22: 743-771.

ROBINSON, P. M. (1982) "On the asymptotic properties of estimators with limited dependent variables." Econometrica 50: 27-42.

ROSSETT, R. N. (1959) "A statistical model of friction in economics." Econometrica 27: 263-267.

――――and F. D. NELSON (1975) "Estimation of the two-limit probit regression model." Econometrica 43: 141-146.

SPECTOR, L. and M. MAZZEO (1980) "Probit analysis and economic education."
Journal of Economic Education 11: 37-44.

TOBIN, J. (1958) "Estimation of relationships for limited dependent variables." Econometrica 26: 24-36.

WEISBERG, H. W. (1978) "Evaluating theories of congressional roll-call voting." American Journal of Political Science 22: 554-557.

JOHN H. ALDRICH is Professor of Political Science at the University of Minnesota. He has taught courses in statistics and formal modeling at the University of Minnesota and at Mighigan State University. His major area of research is the development and testing of models of parties and electoral choice. He has published numerous articles in scholarly journals. He is also the author of Before the Convention (University of Chicago Press, 1980) and co-author of Change and Continuity in the 1980 Elections (Congressional Quarterly Press, rev. ed., 1983, with Paul Abramson and David Rohde).

FORREST D. NELSON is Associate Professor of Economics at the University of Iowa. He has taught courses in statistics and econometrics at the University of Iowa and at California Institute of Technology. His major area of research is methods of analysis for economic models with qualitative and limited dependent variables. Professor Nelson has published numerous articles on theoretical and applied econometrics in scholarly journals, including Econometrica and Journal of Econometrics.